AF574571

Winning
Against the Odds

Winning
Against the Odds

by

Judge Sam Robinson

Library Research Associates Inc.
Monroe, New York
1993

Library Research Associates, Inc.
Dunderberg Road, RD#5, Box 41
Monroe, New York 10950

Library of Congress Cataloging-in-Publication Data:

Robinson, Judge Sam (1899-)
Winning Against the Odds by Sam Robinson
p. 195
ISBN:0-912526-58-0 : $17.50
1. Robinson, Sam, 1899- . 2. Lawyers--Arkansas--Biography. 3. Judges--Arkansas--Biography 4. Arkansas--Social Customs--20th C.
I. Title
KF373.R555A38 1993
340'.092--dc20
[B] 92-29120
CIP

Dedicated to:

My ancestors

who passed on to me the genes
that enabled me to go forward
under the most adverse circumstances.

Table of Contents

Acknowledgment

I want to acknowledge with gratitude the help of Ruth Ann, my wife, who patiently wrote this book in long hand as I dictated it, and then typed it. It was no easy task and without her help there would be no book.

Judge Sam Robinson

Chapter I

The Beginning

Grace Goldstein was not her real name, just the one she used in operating her elaborate, pretentious whorehouse in Hot Springs, Arkansas. She told me her name was Jewel Laverne Grayson. She was charged with conspiracy in connection with a two million dollar mail robbery committed by Alvin Karpis and his gang in Illinois. Later she was also charged with violation of the Mann Act in transporting a female in interstate commerce for immoral purposes. I represented her in these cases, but that is a pretty long episode and I will deal with it later.

I will deal with a fight for life on top of a Mississippi River levee during flood time; with plantation life as it existed more than sixty years ago; with the prosecution and defense of many cases involving life and death; with writing six hundred opinions as a Justice on the Supreme Court of Arkansas; with the courage of Colonel August A. Busch, Jr.; and with hazardous adventures in horse and mule-packing in the Colorado Rockies.

I am now old — very old, having been born in 1899 and am writing this book at the age of ninety three. I started living at a very early age and am still living. What I mean by that is I am doing something besides merely existing.

From time to time I have told Ruth Ann, my wife, about some of the experiences and observations I have had in my lifetime and she has urged me to reduce some of them to writing. Hence, I am undertaking to do so. I don't know whether this will be a series of articles, historical record, biography, or just plain nothing.

Chapter II

Chanticleer Plantation

I was born on Chanticleer Plantation in Chicot County in the southeast corner of Arkansas with two of the county boundaries being the Mississippi River on the east and the State of Louisiana on the south. Chanticleer Plantation lies on the banks of Lake Chicot, formerly a part of the channel of the Mississippi River. It was a big bend at one time and the river cut through the neck of the bend, thus forming a lake on the old riverbed, Lake Chicot.

History tells us that DeSoto, on his journey into the interior, crossed the Mississippi near where the lake is now. He met with misfortune shortly thereafter, never finding his dream which was probably the Hot Springs that gave rise to the spa facilities at the city of Hot Springs, located in the middle of Arkansas. On the return trip through what is now Chicot County, DeSoto died and is said to have been buried there on the banks of the Mississippi River.

Chanticleer adjoins Lake Village, the county seat. It was not large as plantations go, having about twelve hundred acres at the time it was owned by my father. He and his brothers and sisters had inherited the place from their mother, who was Mary Gaines before she married my grandfather, James Forbes Robinson. My father bought out the interests of his brothers and sisters a few years before I was born.

The Gaines family was an illustrious one of Natchez, Mississippi. When Jefferson Davis returned from the Mexican War of 1848, the future president of the Confederacy was entertained at Natchez and welcomed in a speech given by Mary Gaines, a young lady at the time. Davis presented her with a ring which was engraved, "To Mary Gaines — from Jefferson Davis."

Original letter of September 4, 1862
From General D. Sullins to Major James F. Robinson

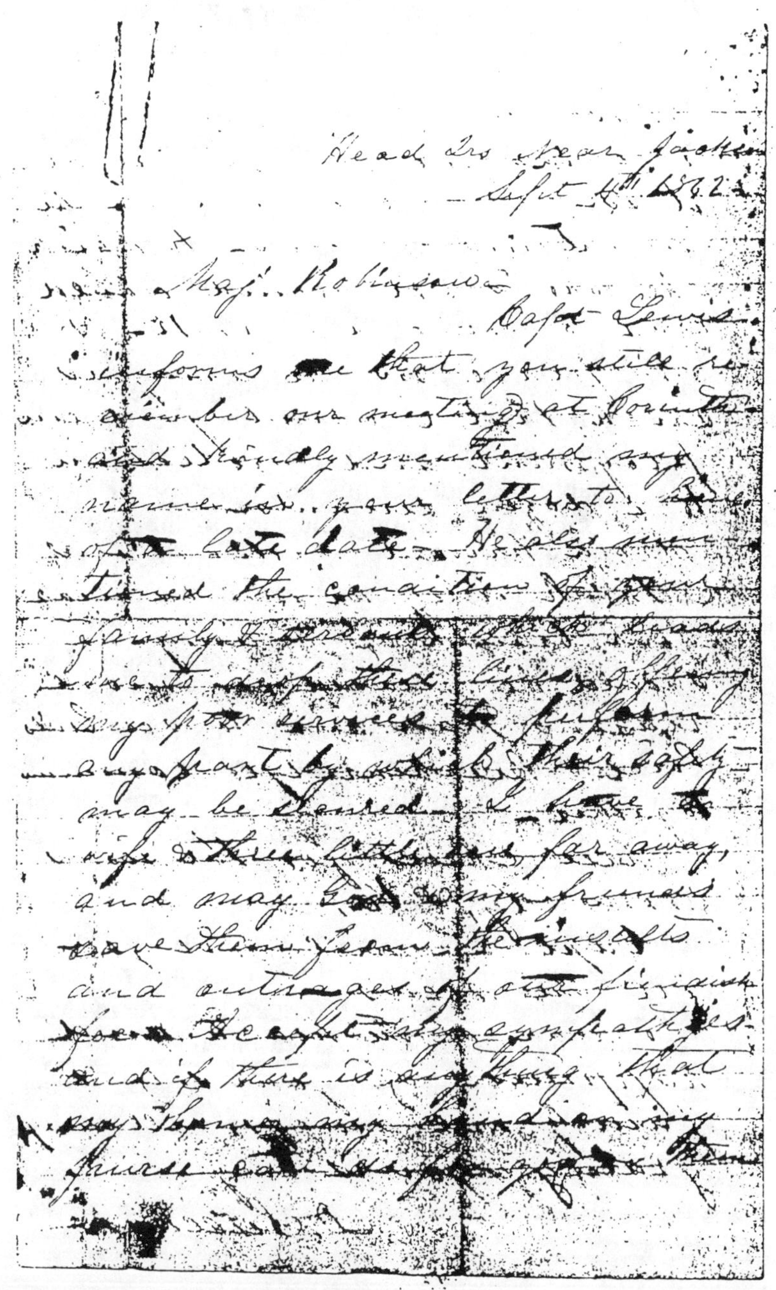

Head Qrs near Jackson
Sept 4th 1862

Maj. Robinson

Capt Lewis informs me that you still remember our meeting at Corinth and kindly mentioned my name in your letters to him of late date. He also mentioned the condition of your family & friends which leave me to accept the lines offering my poor services to perform any part by which their safety may be secured. I have a wife & three little ones far away, and may God & my friends save them from the insults and outrages of our fiendish foe. Accept my sympathies and if there is anything that may [illegible] my friends can [illegible] please do me the favor of allowing me to know what it is— I have a home in the mountains of Tenn— to which she who is left behind would leap to welcome Mrs B— & my place in the army is such that I could give employment and protection to a dozen servants—

From present indications I think likely we will be near your branch of the army— I should be pleased for more reasons than one to see Genls Price & Breckinridge's command together—

Three cheers for the news from Ky & Va,

Capt L— will give you all the news—

To hear of the health and happiness of your self & family will always will [illegible] gratify yours truly—

D. Sull[illegible]

I don't know much about my grand father except that he came from County Clare, Ireland, probably as a teen-ager. He was an educated person, a lawyer, and came down from Philadelphia to Natchez and married my grandmother there. I think Chanticleer was given to them as a wedding present.

There were slaves on Chanticleer and I have seen bills of sale that had been given to my grandfather in connection with the purchase of slaves. When I saw the papers in 1929, they were in the possession of my Aunt Brooksie. It seems like the price of a slave had a good deal to do with the age — or the other way around, the age had a good deal to do with the price.

One bill of sale was for a girl six years of age, and the price was six hundred dollars; another female, sixteen years of age, was sixteen hundred dollars; and a male, twenty-three years of age, was purchased for twenty-three hundred dollars. This could be a coincidence, but it looks like the price was increased one hundred dollars per year.

Grandpa Robinson was a major in the Confederate Army. A letter he received while in Virginia from General D. Sullins sheds a good deal of light on the conditions existing during that period of the war when the Federal soldiers were coming up the Mississippi River. In fact, there was a battle at Ditch Bayou near Lake Village.

The letter reads as follows: (See Plate No. 1 - Sullins)

Head Qrs. Near Jackson
Sept. 4th, 1862

Maj. Robinson -
Capt. Lewis informs me that you still remember our meeting at Corinth - and kindly mentioned my name in your letter, to him, of a late date - He also mentioned the condition of your family & servants, which leads me to drop these lines, offering my poor services to perform any part by which their safety may be secured - I have a wife & three little ones, far away, and may God & my friend save them from the insults and outrages of our fiendish foe - Accept my sympathies - and if there is anything that my home, my hand or my purse can do for you or them please do me the favor of allowing me to know what it is - I have a home in the mountains of

Tenn. - to which she who is left behind would leap to welcome Mrs. R. - & my place in the army is such that I could give employment and protection to a dozen servants -

From present indication I think likely we will be near your branch of the army - I should be pleased for more reasons that one to see Gen'ls Prices's and Breckinridge's command together -

Three cheers for the news from Ky. & Va.

Capt. L. will give you all the news -

To hear of the health and happiness of yourself & family will always gratify.

Yours truly,
/s/D. Sullins

The following letter from General Albert Pike indicates conditions somewhat after the Civil War. It will be noted that General Pike, ordinarily a wealthy man, had only two dollars at the time.

The letter reads as follows: (See Plate No. 2 - Pike)

Washington, D.C., 1st January, 1870

Dear Robinson,

On my return to Memphis I paid out all the money I had received except enough to pay my way to New Orleans and here. The consequence is I am as poor as a church rat, having in the Treasury a little over two dollars. I am sorry for this, because I feel very deeply obliged to you for your kindness and would make any sacrifice to get the money for you. But no money can be borrowed here. If I succeed in getting any fees before April, I will remit. If I do not, I will, I am sure, be able to pay you then. Nobody in Chicot owes me money on whom I can call. Try and manage until April, and I don't think I will fail you then.

All I can tell you about the Drennan (?) Land, is that it was mortgaged by Benjamin Hughes to the R.E. Bk for $30,000 stock, mortgaged on it yet. The numbers I don't remember. I only know that Drennan (?) took under the decree. The record of the mortgage and the decree were then all I ever knew about it.

Truly yours,
/s/ Albert Pike

Jas. F. Robinson, Esq.

Original letter of January 1, 1870
From General Albert Pike to Major James F. Robinson

ALBERT PIKE. ROBERT W. JOHNSON.

PIKE & JOHNSON,

ATTORNEYS AND COUNSELLORS,

PRACTICE IN THE SUPREME COURT AND COURT OF CLAIMS,

AND ATTEND TO BUSINESS, CLAIMS, OR ACCOUNTS BEFORE CONGRESS OR THE DEPARTMENTS,

Office: 217 F Street, opposite U. S. Treasury.

P. O. Box 753.

Washington D. C. 1st January 1870.

Dear Robinson

On my return to Memphis, I paid out all the money I had received except enough to pay my way to New Orleans and here. The consequence is that I am as poor as a Church Rat; having in the Treasury a little over two dollars. I am sorry for this, because I feel very deeply obliged to you for your kindness and would make any sacrifice to get [illegible]

[illegible]

in getting any fees before April, I will [illegible] funds, I am sure, be able to pay you then. Nobody in [illegible] owes me money, on whom I can call. Try and manage until April, and I don't think I will fail you then.

All I can tell you about the [illegible] land, is that it was mortgaged by Benjamin Hughes to the R. E. Bk, for "[illegible] mortgaged premises for money borrowed by him; and the lien for the bond liability as it was. The numbers I don't remember. I only know that [illegible] under the decree. The record of the mortgage and the decree will show all I ever knew about it.

Truly yours

Jas. F. Robinson Esq

Albert Pike

Original letter of 31, 1865
From Robert E. Lee to James Forbes Robinson →

Lexington Va: 31 Oct '65

My dear Sir

I rec'd last evening your letter of the 16th Inst: & enclose a Circular of Washington College, which I hope will give you the information you desire.

You will observe that a Class supplementary to the Freshman, has been organized, to suit the cases of such Students to whom you refer, & to enable them by diligence to take up with the Freshmen, & proceed with them next year in the Sophomore Course.

A Student can take any Course of Studies he may select, for which he is prepared, & enter at any time, if able to keep up with the class in which he recites.

The annual expense of the term, varies from $175. to $300. The route from Memphis is either by the Tenn: & Va: R.R. to Lynchburg, Va: & thence by Canal to Lexington; or by the Ohio river, or R.R. by Albany, Cincinnati & Cumd. Balt & O. R.R. via Baltimore & Washington, to Staunton, & thence by Stage. I do not know the comparative advantages since a resumption of travel. Previous to the war, the Tenn & Va: R.R. was the preferable.

Students can take rooms in College, & board in the town of Lexington, or lodge & board in Lexington as they prefer. The session continues from 1st Oct to 1st July.

Respectfully your obt Servt

R E Lee

Mr James H. Robinson

After the Civil War, Robert E. Lee was the President of Washington University, later known as Washington and Lee. Grandpa wrote to him about sending one or more of his children to that college and in reply, General Lee sent Grandpa a copy of what a student was required to know upon entering the University.

In these days many students are not as well-educated when they finish college as they had to be just to enter Washington College at the time of which I write. The letter reads as follows: (See Plate No.3 - Lee)

Lexington, VA: 31st '65

My dear Sir,

I received last week your letter of the 16th inst: I enclose a circular of Washington College, which I hope will give you the information you desire.

You will observe that a clafs supplementary to the Freshman has been organized, to suit the cases of such students to whom you refer, & to enable them by diligence to take up with the Freshmen & proceed with them next year in the Sophomore Course.

A student can take any course of studies he may select, for which he is prepared, & enter at any time, if able to keep up with the clafs in which he recites.

The annual expense of the term, varies from $275, to $300. The route from Memphis is either by the Tenn & VA: R.R. to Lynchburg, VA: & thence by Canal to Lexington; or by the Ohio river, or R.R. by Albany, Cincinnati O. and Bal & O. R.R. via Baltimore & Washington, to Staunton: & thence by stage. I do not know the comparative advantages since resumptin (?) of travel. Previous to the war, the Tenn & VA: R.R. was the preferable.

Students can take rooms in College & board in the town of Lexington, or lodge & board in Lexington as they prefer. The sefsion continues from Oct: to Jul.

Very respt your obt Srvt, R.E.Lee

Mr. JamesF. Robinson

The originals of these letters are in the possession of my son, Sam Robinson, Jr..

In the early 1890's, Grandpa Robinson was appointed Chancery Judge for the First Chancery District of Arkansas by

WASHINGTON COLLEGE,

Lexington, Virginia,.., 1865

THE FACULTY.

GEN. ROBERT E. LEE, President,

——— ——— ——— Professor of Mental and Moral Science,

J. L. CAMPBELL, A. M., Professor of Physical Science,

A. L. NELSON, A. M., Professor of Mathematics,

JAMES J. WHITE, A. M., Professor of Greek,

C. J. HARRIS, A. M., Professor of Latin,

PROFESSOR THOMAS M. SEMMES, will teach the Classes in French.

COURSE OF STUDY.

FRESHMAN CLASS.

LATIN.—Cæsar—Arnold's Nepos—Cicero de Senectute—Arnold's Prose Composition—Zumpt's Grammar—Geography of Ancient Italy and Gaul.

GREEK.—Xenophon's Anabasis—Kuhner's Elementary Grammar—Geography of Ancient Greece.

MATHEMATICS.—Davies' Bourdon's Algebra—Davies' Legendre.

SOPHOMORE CLASS.

LATIN.—Livy—Cicero, Epistolæ ad Diversos—Virgil—Zumpt's & Madvig's Grammar—Exercises in Composition by Professor.

GREEK.—Xenophon's Memorabilia—Demosthenes de Corona, Euripides—Kuhner's Elementary Greek Grammar.

MATHEMATICS.—Plane and Spherical Trigonometry—Surveying (Davies')—Descriptive Geometry (Davies'.)

JUNIOR CLASS.

LATIN.—Tacitus' Annals—Latin Composition—same Grammars as above.

GREEK.—Sophocles—Kuhner's Greek Grammar—Exercises by Professor.

MATHEMATICS.—Analytical Geometry, (Smith's Biot)—Courtenay's Calculus.

*PHYSICAL SCIENCE.—Chemistry (Fowne's)—Agriculture (Campbell's.)

MENTAL PHILOSOPHY, LOGIC AND RHETORIC.

SENIOR CLASS.

LATIN.—Horace—Terence—Lucretius de Rerum Natura—Exercises in Composition—Roman History.

GREEK.—Thucydides—Homer's Iliad—Greek Literature (Brown's)—Exercises by Professor—Ancient Geography (Long's Atlas.)

MATHEMATICS.—Mechanics (Smith's.)

PHYSICAL SCIENCE.—Geology (Hitchcock's)—Astronomy (Herschell's.)

MORAL SCIENCE—POLITICAL ECONOMY—EVIDENCES OF CHRISTIANITY.

NOTE.—Exercises in Composition and Declamation are required of all the Classes, and, Original Orations of the Senior Class.

FRENCH.—Bolmar's Levizac's Grammar—Fasquelle's French Course—Collot's Dramatic French Reader—Gil Blas.

☞ The study of Modern Languages is at the option of the Student.

Applicants for admission into the Freshman Class should be familiar with the Latin and Greek Grammars, and have acquired a good degree of facility in Translation. They should be acquainted with Arithmetic and the Elements of Algebra.

☞ Students, who do not wish to take the full College Course, are allowed to recite with the regular classes in any of the above studies, for which the Faculty shall judge them competent; it being required that each Student shall have at least three daily recitations.

☞ With a view to accommodate young men, whose education has been interrupted by the late war, a class supplementary to the Freshman will be organized, in which will be taught the Elements of Latin, Greek and Mathematics. This class is not intended for boys.

EXPENSES.—Tuition, $50. All other fees, including room-rent, $25. Boarding from $15 to $20 per month, for meals alone. French, extra, $20.

Students proposing to lodge in College will have to provide furniture for their own rooms.

☞ Students may reach Lexington by stage from Staunton, or by canal from Lynchburg.

TEXT-BOOKS can be procured in Lexington.

The Session opens October 2d, and continues to June 20th.

---

*Arrangements have been made to renew the Chemical and Philosophical Apparatus.

Governor James P. Eagle. Years later when I first started practice as a young lawyer in Little Rock, a Mr. Hogue was still practicing and told me of visiting Chanticleer as a guest of my grandfather. Mr. Hogue spoke of the fine hospitality and especially remembered that each morning a fire, which had been laid in the fireplace in his bedroom, was lit and that his freshly shined shoes were outside the bedroom door. This home burned before I was born and we lived in a much smaller home, although of good size.

All of Grandpa Robinson's children were well-educated and I believe that Uncle Jack, who was a Civil Engineer, graduated from Yale. He went to Gunnison, Colorado at an early age and remained there for the rest of his life.

My mother's father was Dr. S.R. Dunn of Greenville, Mississippi, and was a graduate of Jefferson Medical College in Philadelphia. Before her marriage my mother's mother was Amanda Rucks; the Rucks family were all highly-educated plantation owners of the Mississippi Delta.

I mention all the foregoing background because, in comparison, the course my life took is unbelievable. Early in my life my father became a complete and total alcoholic. He lost Chanticleer and everything, including his family, by reason of alcohol. And, finally, it killed him too.

I remember one occasion while we were still living on the plantation, a colored man was driving four mules taking a load of cotton from our plantation to a gin near Lake Village. There was a wagon sheet across the top of the cotton and Papa had crawled underneath the sheet because he was trying to slip off to go to town and get some whiskey. Mama went out there with a pistol in her hand and made the driver stop the wagon and Papa came crawling out. Shortly after that episode Papa was forced to sell Chanticleer and he sold it to a Mr. Alcorn, who was from Mississippi.

After the loss of Chanticleer Plantation, we moved into Lake Village. There was enough money left over after all the debts were paid for Papa to build us a home there. But it wasn't long before it too was gone, perhaps less than a year. I was 5 years of age.

Chapter III

Lake Village Years: 1904-1905

Lake Village was a typical small southern town in 1904, with dirt streets, wooden sidewalks, and a railroad depot. There were several dry goods stores: Ebstein's, Rosenwag's, McClung's, Bunker's, and also Forte's grocery store.

There was a vast difference in the manner of operating a store at that time and the way the stores are run today. During those early days a customer did not go in and pick out what he wanted. Everyone was waited on by someone working in the store and the merchandise was kept on shelves behind counters.

Grocery stores were handled pretty well the same way, selling flour, meal, beans, canned and bottled goods. There were no fresh vegetables in these stores and no meat. There were meat markets separate and apart from grocery stores and the fresh vegetables were bought directly from someone in the country.

The meat market in Lake Village was run by a Chinaman named "Wolf" and his Caucasian wife. The fact that Mrs. Wolf, a very pretty brunette, was married to a Chinaman did not bring about any unfavorable talk regarding her, although at that time she might not have been accepted into high society. And there definitely was "high society" in the small town of Lake Village. An expert horsewoman, Mrs. Wolf was talked about because she rode "astride" (like a man), while wearing a riding skirt, when other women of that time still rode side saddle.

Mrs. Wolf would buy cattle in the country. I say, "cattle," actually I don't think she ever handled more than one at a time as

I never saw her driving more than one head. She would drive it to a slaughter house they had where it would be slaughtered and the meat taken to their meat market. There it was put in a large cooler which was kept cold by ice shipped in on the railroad.

The "high society" that I mentioned, was composed of delta people "born" into it. Money didn't count. It didn't make any difference how poor a person might be. If he was born "right," of the right people, he was considered of that class and accepted. On the other hand a person might be wealthy, but if he wasn't born "right" - that is - if he did not come from a line of gentility, he simply was not accepted. The people of this social strata were well educated, well read, and would have felt at home in any mansion or castle on the face of the earth. They had good manners and if a person did not have good table manners, he definitely did not belong.

Another characteristic of this class of people was their pride. Although practically all of these families had lost everything as a result of the Civil War, accepting charity was unthinkable and many, like mama, took steps to keep secret their real position.

All of my relatives were of this social order, and many of them lived in Chicot County: Gaines, Chapman, Carlton, Haynes, Robinson, Simms, Davis, Yearger. In fact, I was kin to a large portion of the population of Lake Village. All of these kinspeople recognized this kinship. They referred to each other as "Cousin so-and-so" although they may have been very distant cousins or didn't even remember just how the relationship came about.

The delta people of whom I speak did not perform any manual labor. They did not know how and were not capable of doing it. I doubt very seriously that any, including my relatives, ever drove a nail (certainly not many nails), or ever sawed off a board or tried to spade up a garden in their entire lives. On the other hand, they were lawyers, judges, doctors, writers, artists and plantation owners. They held all the political offices and in rare instances were in the mercantile business. Generally speaking, however, they were not good business people. Lake Village in 1922, with a population of approximately 1500, had 15 lawyers.

The people in the town who did not belong in this society did not resent it, it was just an accepted condition. All of these people could work together, would like each other and be real good friends, but socially they did not mingle. Breeding was everything. As time passed, however, money became more important than breeding.

Mr. Bunker, the owner of one of the dry goods stores, had several children who were just about grown at the time we moved from the plantation. The two boys were Nelson and Lamar. The daughter, Lyda, married H.L. Hunt, who also lived in Lake Village.

Hunt was a natural gambler at heart and an expert poker player. This was big poker playing country, and it was not unheard of for a plantation to be lost in a poker game. When oil was discovered near El Dorado in the early 20's, Hunt went there. Ed Beavis, a long time professional gambler in Little Rock (and a friend of mine), told me that he and Johnny Harding, Beavis' partner, also went to El Dorado. They opened a gambling house and Hunt worked for them in this gambling house for quite a while.

Then Hunt got into dealing in oil leases and royalties. He made a lot of money at El Dorado and when the East Texas oil around Long View was discovered, Hunt went there. Again, he did well in the oil business, became very wealthy and moved to Dallas where he continued his oil operations. At one time, he was considered to be the wealthiest man in the United States.

Hunt's sons, Nelson Bunker Hunt and Lamar Hunt, were named after Lyda's two brothers. Years later, Lyda's nephew, Nelson Bunker, Jr. ("June") and I were in the cattle business together for some time. June was a fine man, easy to work with and I liked him very much.

Along with the dry goods stores, Lake Village also had Tom Henderson's General Store and several saloons; one across from the courthouse and another, run by Bill and Joe Frame, across from the depot.

By today's standards, Lake Village would be considered a violent town and practically everyone carried a pistol. Two incidents will serve to illustrate. There was some consorting between white men and Negro women, primarily in colored whorehouses that were patronized only by white men. At a dance in a whorehouse down by the depot, some trouble broke out between one of the white men and the Negro orchestra leader. They both pulled guns. Then a white man, Frank Anderson, a big strapping fellow who was well-liked and had good family connections, stepped between the two men trying to stop the trouble. He was shot and killed by the bandleader who was shooting at the other man. Then others started shooting.

One of those present in the whorehouse at the time of the shooting was a local lawyer and he had one of the whores sitting on his lap. A stray bullet went through the woman and entered the lawyer, but both recovered from their wounds. The lawyer later moved to Little Rock where he became a prominent attorney statewide. The Negro bandleader was arrested and put in jail. The next day a mob formed to lynch him.

Although not a peace officer, my father did everything he could to prevent the lynching. He confronted the mob in front of the jail trying to dissuade them from carrying out their intentions, but it did no good. They broke into the jail, took the man down to a big cottonwood tree on the lake bank right across from the courthouse and hanged him. Ironically, this was the same tree used by Negroes to hang three white men during the aftermath of the Civil War. My grandfather, James Forbes Robinson, was the one who cut them down and buried them.

The second incident involved a beautiful young woman, Helen Cook Crews, and her husband, Charlie Crews. One evening my mother and father were preparing to go to a dance when word came that Helen had been killed while she and Charlie were getting ready to go to the same dance. Charlie's story was that his pistol had fallen out of his pocket and discharged upon hitting the floor, that the bullet hit Helen and killed her. There was not much sympathy for Charlie and many questioned his story about the supposed accident. People who carry a revolver keep an empty chamber under the hammer just to prevent this type of thing. Most of the Lake Village citizens questioned why Charlie didn't. It was not long after, that someone killed Charlie in one of the Lake Village saloons. A lot of people thought it was a hired killing, including myself. The man who did the killing was never brought to trial.

During that time, epidemics of yellow fever broke out periodically throughout the delta country. It was infectious and fatal and people died by the score. When I was about five, an epidemic broke out in nearby Louisiana and people tried to come into Arkansas to get away from it. Some slipped up the Mississippi river in boats trying to cross the state line but the National Guard was called out to prevent this.

One day while I was in our front yard, about a dozen men on horseback came by in a dead run, all armed with shotguns or rifles. There had been a report that a steamboat from Louisiana was coming upriver and was going to attempt to land at Sunnyside Plantation in Arkansas near the end of Lake Chicot, a plantation later owned by my friend, James Mohead. The men on horseback were going to prevent the boat from landing and they would have killed anyone attempting to get off that boat.

Later, of course, it was discovered that the fever was transmitted by the bite of the yellow fever mosquito, which was exterminated. I have never known how they exterminated the yellow fever mosquito without exterminating all mosquitoes, just like the Texas Fever tick — which caused great losses in cattle — they eliminated it, but not all ticks.

We had relatives on the Gaines' side of the family who lived in Hot Springs. There was no fever there and our family left Lake Village by train to stay with these relatives until the epidemic was over. Hot Springs is located in the hill country away from the river lowlands, and was, therefore, free from yellow fever.

On our way to Hot Springs, we stopped overnight at the Capitol Hotel in Little Rock and had dinner in the dining room on the first floor of the north east portion of the hotel, now known as "Ashleys." We had corn-on-the-cob and the corncob holders fascinated me as I hadn't seen any before. Years later the hotel was greatly run-down and, in one period, was used largely by prostitutes. In recent years it has been restored as a historical landmark and when I visited Little Rock early in 1985, some eighty years after my first experience with the corncob holders, I ate in that same dining room and it looked remarkably the same. After the epidemic we returned to Lake Village.

There were about thirteen wild donkeys running loose around Lake Village; about ten jennies, two jacks and one that had been gelded. They had been obtained in the west by a Dr. Connelly who lived at Lake Village, apparently for some purpose that did not work out. In time they were just turned loose to fend for themselves, which they did in a most able manner. I never saw one of them in poor condition.

These donkeys were pretty well-known to everybody in the community and they had even been given names. One of the jacks was bigger than the other and had kind of a red back, so was called "Red." The smaller one was light-colored and where in the world the name came from I don't know, but he was called "Dusenberry." The gelding was called "One-Eyed Johnny" because he had lost one eye from an injury.

I decided that I would catch the gelding to see if I could ride him. I'd patched up a bridle for him and much to my surprise, he wasn't very hard to catch. I wasn't old enough to go to school yet and wasn't big enough to get up on him without a log or a high place. So I got him up to a bank where I could get on him and rode off — my first time ever on a donkey. He didn't do a thing. He rode good and I claimed One-Eyed Johnny for mine. No one objected and I kept him for the time we lived in Lake Village.

Sometimes he got out and went back with the other donkeys. The two jacks would fight him and bite him up quite a bit, mostly on his back legs above the hocks. When I caught him up again, which I did real soon, I put black axle grease on the places where he was bitten and he healed right away. I learned a lot from One-Eyed Johnny and he may have learned something from me, and when we left Lake Village I left him with the other donkeys.

From as far back as I can remember, I was free to do anything that I was able to do. I cannot remember ever being told, "not to do this" or, "not to do that." And I did just what I pleased.

One day, while off by myself paddling in Lake Chicot in a batteau (a boat which is flat on the bottom and both ends but shaped to make it ride easily in the water) I discovered a trot line that had been abandoned. It was about one hundred feet long, with hooks tied to it every two feet, and was made of small cotton twine called "stagen," which was very strong. One end of the trot line was tied to a cypress tree growing in the water near the bank with a weight on the other end of the line out in the lake. I immediately dug up some worms to bait the hooks and, thereafter for quite some time, I ran the trot line every day. I paddled the batteau to where the line was tied to the tree and, using the line to pull the boat along, took the fish from the hooks, rebaiting them at the same time. I took the fish I caught home, some of them to be given to neighbors as I had caught too many for us to eat.

I caught quite a few catfish that way and on one occasion there was one on the line I could not get in the boat. I was only five or six years old at the time. I could just get it up to where I could see its head and it was the biggest catfish I have ever seen to this day. His head was about eight inches wide and he had apparently swallowed a small fish that was already hooked on the line. He finally pulled loose and swam away.

At this time I was a good swimmer and no-one worried about me being out on the lake by myself. In fact, sometimes I went out on the lake paddling a dugout, which I found where it had been washed up on the bank. A dugout is much harder to control than a batteau as it has a round bottom, more like a canoe. It is made from the whole trunk of a tree, the log being shaped on the outside by someone being skillful with an ax and an adz. The log was hollowed out with the same tools and I think that sometimes a controlled fire was used in the "hollowing out" process. A dugout would ride lightly in the water but would turn over easily.

About that time my father gave me a single-barrel twelve-gauge shotgun and, at that early age, I learned to shoot it although it had quite a kick. Mostly I shot birds and pulldoos. A pulldoo is a duck that is also called a "coot." It has a head like a chicken and it is not fit to eat.

I got my first job working for Mr. Fagen Thompkins who owned a dairy, and to this day there has never been a time of more than a few days that I haven't had a job of some kind.

Having learned to ride on One-Eyed Johnny, I was given the job of riding out to the pasture in the evenings on one of Mr. Thompkin's horses to get the cattle and bring them in to be milked. They stayed in the barn at night and were milked again in the morning before being put back out to pasture.

I delivered milk too. Mr. Thompkins had two horses used for that purpose, one of them a big, tall bay horse that just wouldn't get fat and we called him "Bones." I would drive him or an old grey mare hitched to a one-horse spring wagon — easy riding, as well as easy on the load. At some places on the route the customers were quite a distance apart and, on more than one occasion, that mare left while I was delivering the milk to the house. But she always stopped at the next place on the route except one time when she kept moving ahead of me for three or four places down the line before I could catch up with her.

While working there I had my first experience breaking a horse. Mr. Thompkins had a real good three-year-old filly and, in his absence, I took it upon myself to break her. Having been raised around the barn, she was gentle but had never been ridden. I managed to get a bridle on her and led her up to a feed trough where I was able to put a lightweight army-type saddle on her. I cinched up the saddle but then she broke loose, ran to the back of the lot and did a real good job of bucking trying to get rid of that saddle. After I caught her, I brought her back to the barn, took the saddle off and led her up to the feed trough again. I got on her bareback and she didn't buck. I never put a saddle on her again and she never did buck again. I would ride her driving in the cattle and also to school where I was in the first grade. But Mr. Thompkins soon made me quit riding her to school, because I had to leave her tied up all day.

I don't remember just exactly what Mr. Thompkins was paying me but, as I recall, it was about a dollar a week. It wasn't much but it helped out at home where things were getting worse all the time. My mother, a fine pianist, heard that she could probably get a job in one of the new motion picture houses in Little Rock and finally decided that we'd move.

Chapter IV

Paper Route and Red-Light Deliveries: Little Rock

1906-1917

When we moved to Little Rock, we took the Missouri Pacific passenger train. It was called the "Cannonball" because it could attain the fantastic speed of forty miles per hour. When we got off the train at the depot in Little Rock, we had to walk up a long flight of stairs to get to the waiting room and we came out on ground level. I was not familiar with "hills" as Chicot County is flat, and it was hard for me to understand how you could walk up on one side and come out on level ground on the other side.

Mama did get a job playing piano at a moving picture theater in Little Rock. Mr. Frank Strong, a former sheriff of Chicot County, had moved his family to Little Rock some hears prior to our moving there. Mama made arrangements with the Strongs to rent part of their home, a large, two-story house at 1310 Battery Street where we had the upper floor. The house, although remodeled, is still there.

At this time, moving pictures were only in black and white, no color and no sound. The theater owners considered it good, or perhaps necessary, to add a musical background to the picture, music that fit the mood of the picture. Sometimes the music would consist of just a piano, and other times there would be an orchestra — about a five piece orchestra, usually some combination of these instruments: Piano, violin, cello, bass fiddle, coronet, clarinet and drums.

The working hours for the musicians were long and hard. Mama went to work at 1 o'clock in the afternoon and got off at 10 at night, 6 days a week. Therefore we did not see much of her, and there were four of us children. Lucile was 10, I was 7, Harry was 4 and Gallie was a babe in arms (usually Lucile's). During all that time I have no memory of ever sitting at the table for a family meal together.

It was 1906. Automobiles were becoming more popular and there were quite a few electric ones which looked like buggies with the top up. I've often wondered why the electric car wasn't developed like the gas engine automobile. Perhaps someone had some oil to sell.

These electric cars were one seat, two passenger cars, mostly driven by women. There was no steering wheel, but the driver steered with a horizontal bar situated in front of the driver. The power was furnished by storage batteries which were recharged by the city's electrical system. These electric cars were the only ones that most women could operate at the time because to start one it was only necessary to turn on a switch. Cars powered by gasoline had to be cranked by hand, and this was beyond the capacity of most women. For some reason, I never recall seeing an electric car driven by a man.

Main Street in Little Rock was paved with cobblestones when we first moved there. But in about 1912 the stones were torn up and the street was paved with creosoted wooden blocks about twice the size of an ordinary brick. The blocks were not very satisfactory; water got underneath them, washed them out, and they would pile up in low places in the street. So they removed the blocks and paved the street with a hard surface material.

I soon met a boy who carried a paper route and it wasn't long before I, too, had a route. It began at Sixteenth and Park where the papers were delivered in the Gazette's truck, probably the first of its kind in Arkansas. The delivery truck was chain-driven and had carbide lights that stuck out on each side of the windshield as well as in front of the truck, and the top of the lights got very hot. One time I was getting out of the truck and badly burned my elbow on one of them. The scars stayed for years.

Several routes fanned out from that point and mine covered the area from 16th and Park up to Eighth Street and over to the railroad. Through the years I carried various routes. The number of papers ranged from about eighty-five on the smallest route to about one hundred and seventy-five on the largest. The pay was two dollars and sixty cents a week if you didn't get any complaints or "kicks," as we called them.

It's almost impossible to carry a route without getting any "kicks" in a week. Sometimes you would forget to throw the paper or maybe you would throw it too far and it would land on the roof of the house. Other times the paper would be stolen or sometimes a dog would carry it off. The company took off twenty-five cents for the first "kick" and ten cents for all those after that. So, I usually made a little over two dollars a week. After I finished my route for the Gazette each Sunday, I also sold other newspapers on Main Street in downtown Little Rock. These were the St. Louis papers: the *Globe*, the *Post*, the *Dispatch* and sometimes the *Republic*.

The Sunday paper was much bigger, therefore much heavier than the daily papers. One of the ways the paper boys handled this problem was with the help of the streetcar motormen. We would put bundles of papers on the streetcars and the motorman would drop them off at specified places on the route, usually real close to where the previous bundle had run out. We would give the motorman a five- cent paper for doing that. I also used a little two-wheel push wagon on Sundays to help with the heavy loads.

A warning message was stamped on the front of the funny papers, the outside pages of the *Gazette's* Sunday edition. The message offered a five-dollar reward for information on anyone "offering for sale this subscriber's paper." One Sunday I laid in wait for the person who had been stealing papers from an apartment house at Third and Cumberland after I had delivered them. Sure enough, I didn't have to wait long before I saw a boy about my size go onto the porch of the apartment house and take two papers. I ran him down, took him to the paper office and collected my reward. Five dollars was a real bundle of money in those days!

The *Gazette* had a lot to do with my life. I carried routes in various parts of the city during that seven years. Later, as a lawyer in private practice and as Prosecuting Attorney, I was frequently involved in cases of public interest. The *Gazette* is the oldest paper west of the Mississippi River and has always been highly regarded by its peers and by the public. It is a good newspaper and it always treated me fairly.

But a newspaper can give you hell, as I found out, by running a story that is truthful while still putting you in an unfavorable light. One female reporter took a dislike to me while I was Prosecuting Attorney and did this whenever she could. I went to see Mr. Ned Heiskel, the owner, and pointed out to him what was being done. he promptly put a stop to it and that reporter was not with the *Gazette* very much longer. Mr. Heiskel passed away quite a few years ago, but his good work and the highly-respected traditions of the *Gazette* were carried on by his son-in-law, Hugh Patterson. Hugh always wanted to do what was just, fair and right.

When school opened that first year in Little Rock, I went to Centennial School at Sixteenth and Battery and entered the second grade. I finished that year all the while carrying my paper route, each day getting up at 4 o'clock in the morning. When the next session of school began, I started the third grade, but that lasted only a couple of months. I decided to quit and get a full-time job as things had gotten real tough at home. Mama could hardly make a go of it playing the piano. She wasn't paid much and with four kids, rent, groceries and everything else, it didn't go far. Miss Massey, my teacher, tried to keep me in school but I quit anyhow, just walked off and left.

The Gus Blass Dry Goods Company, later simply called "Blass's," and still later acquired by "Dillards," was the largest department store in Arkansas. It was the first place I went to inquire about a job and sure enough, I was hired as a cash boy although the job had nothing to do with cash. It was mostly running errands and my salary was two dollars a week. This, and the money from the paper route, helped quite a bit at home. Almost the whole time I worked at Blass's, I continued to carry the paper route. I got up at four in the morning to do this, seven days a week. When the weather was very cold, I used matches to warm my hands. Another form of income came from picking up beer bottles in the alleys and selling them to a saloon for fifteen cents a dozen.

When I first went to work at Blass's, the store opened at eight o'clock in the morning and closed at six o'clock in the evening except Saturdays when it stayed open until ten at night. About the year 1912 a big circus ended its season in Little Rock and paid off all its employees. The store stayed open until three o'clock in the morning on that occasion to get as much of the circus business as it could.

Mr. Gus Blass was a fine man loved by everyone. One day I was standing near where a traveling salesman, or as they were then called, a "drummer," was trying to sell Mr. Gus some blue chambray work shirts. They were standing by a table on which our shirts were displayed and were arguing as to which shirts were the best, those the drummer was trying to sell to Mr. Gus or those already on the table. Finally, Mr. Gus turned to me saying, "Come here, boy," and held one of each shirt. He asked me which of the two was best and I had enough judgment to say ours was. Mr. Gus patted me on the head and said, "Some day you will be governor!"

Back in those days much of the merchandise that was purchased by customers was delivered. Horse drawn delivery wagons went out in the morning and in the afternoon on regular delivery routes. In addition, there were deliveries made by boys who were known as special delivery boys, delivering purchases that couldn't wait for the regular delivery wagon. We would take whatever the customer ordered to their houses by way of streetcars. The store would furnish streetcar tickets, or sometimes money — a dime to ride the streetcar round trip. Many times I walked a long distance both ways to save the ten cents.

The red-light district in Little Rock was quite extensive, extending east on Markham Street on both sides of the street for several blocks and also east on Second Street. During that time, the old State Capitol Building on Cumberland, which has since been restored to its original condition, was a whorehouse.

One of the best parts of being a special delivery boy was delivering to Little Rock's red-light district. All the merchandise ordered from these "houses" was sent special delivery C.O.D. Those women generally tipped you a quarter while other people only tipped a nickel or a dime. For the most part, the women were in their twenties and pretty. This is understandable as a homely one would not do much business when there were pretty ones to pick from.

The "houses" were of different classes, and some were more expensive than others. I was about 12 years old and I knew about these things because I frequently delivered packages to all of them at all times of the day and on Saturday nights.

One house, know as "Genevieve and Dorothy's," was one of the most expensive places. The furnishings were definitely better. But perhaps the leading house, if there was such a thing, was operated by Bernice Howard and had the reputation for being a real good house. it was located at 312 1/2 east Markham, a short distance from where the newspaper, the *Arkansas Democrat*, was located at east Markham and Cumberland.

There was also a large red-light district in North Little Rock, and I delivered packages there as well. One of these was operated by Mabel Ervin, a mulatto and all the women in the house were colored, but it was patronized by white men. Often it would be near closing time when I left on a Saturday night delivery to one of the houses, most of which occupied the second floor of business buildings in the wholesale district.

The arrangement of the rooms of these houses was pretty much the same. The entrance to the places over the business buildings was by a stairway leading up from the street with a red light over it. Usually on the globe of the red light was the name of the place, such as "Genieve and Dorothy" or "Bernice Howard." At the top of the stairway was a doorway opening into a hall that went the length of the building with rooms adjacent to the hallway.

The first room to the right or the left of the hall was large, about the size of two ordinary rooms. This is where the men would first go or be directed by one of the women when they arrived at the house. Here they would meet the girls, pick out one they liked and perhaps dance a while (there was always a player piano) and of course, do some drinking. Many times the men were drunk when they arrived in a house or got drunk in the parlor, as the room I have described was called.

In the "better" houses, the girls were not allowed to drink alcoholic beverages though the men were urged to buy them drinks, which were expensive compared to the prices in saloons. The girls drank what were called "B" drinks which consisted of nothing but colored water. And if it was a beer, it was the same thing usually with a napkin wrapped around the bottle so the man couldn't see the contents.

All of these things I could see and hear from where I would be sitting on a bench in the hallway, waiting to see if the girl to whom I had delivered the merchandise would keep it. If she did, she paid me the money. If not, I returned the merchandise to the store. Sometimes I had to wait a long time for the women to get around to deciding if the merchandise was what they wanted — especially if it was a busy night for them. I would then have to walk home, about one and a half miles, if I had missed the last streetcar which left downtown at midnight. I believe it was in 1915 that the red-light district in Little Rock was closed.

Many a Saturday night I missed the "lineup," as the midnight gathering of the streetcars was called, and walked home taking the C.O.D. money with me as the store was long closed. But I didn't mind, the good tips more than made up for the trouble. And in all of the years that I had to be in virtually every section of the city at every time of day and night, I never had any reason to be afraid or had any trouble, except one time. Early one morning delivering papers when I was about 13 or 14, a black youth, bigger and older than I, accosted me with the intention of beating me up. I had a good pocket knife that I pulled from my pocket, opened the blade and that was the end of the matter. The boy left in a hurry.

There were several gangs of boys in the city: the Markham and Cross Gang, the 12th and Battery Gang, the East 22nd Street Gang, and the downtown gang called the Dirty Dozen. The gangs were made up of neighborhood boys who merely ganged together and did things together. But they were no problem to the police and did not, as a gang, commit crimes or cause trouble. There was no violence in the city as there is today and there was absolutely no necessity for having security guards at schools.

Since I was downtown so much, I came in contact with the boys who belonged to the Dirty Dozen. At that time I was somewhere between ten and fourteen years of age. I was never a member of the gang, but I knew them, they knew me and we were friends. The gang would hang out under the free bridge that crossed the Arkansas River at the end of Main Street. Sometimes I would go down there on my lunch hour and we would all go swimming in the river. That section of the river wasn't very clean because there was a large open sewer that dumped its contents not very far upstream from the bridge,. as evidenced by the many condoms that floated by as we swam.

We challenged each other to do stunts and one of the favorite challenges was to see if you could swim out to the first pier and back, quite a distance without being taken downstream by the current. Most of us were good swimmers and not one of us ever drowned.

During my teen-age years I belonged to the YMCA and regularly went there at night to participate in gymnastics and other sports. Walking about five miles each morning while carrying a heavy load of papers and going to the YMCA at night, I built a good, strong body that has stood me in good stead to this day. At ninety years of age I could still ride my horse twenty miles in the mountains.

Most of the boys in the Dirty Dozen got in trouble sooner or later. I remember the names of some of the boys: Tommy

Brewer, Jimmy O'Brien and Nub Henderson who had one hand cut off at the wrist. Years later, when I was Prosecuting Attorney of the Sixth Judicial District, I handled cases involving some of these men. Why did I go a different direction? Somehow I knew my people didn't do those things.

From time to time I worked in various departments at Blass's: As a special delivery boy, a bundle wrapper, for a long time in the auditing department and finally a salesman.

As a cashier, when I was about fourteen years of age, I came up twelve dollars short at the end of one day. It made me physically ill. With no warning, I vomited all over my desk and went home sick. Some of the lady clerks were nice enough to clean it up for me. The next day the store sent word that a check for seven dollars and a five-dollar bill had slipped behind the drawer in the cash register.

My job in the auditing department was filing sales tickets and I learned a whole lot including a good deal about figures. When I was seventeen years old, a fellow gave a check for seventy-five dollars for merchandise in my department and his check turned out to be no good. although I did not wait on the man, I remembered him. The check was drawn on a bank in Carlisle, Arkansas, and Mr. Benson, the department manager who had okayed the check, asked me to go there to see if I could find the man and collect for it.

I went to Carlisle on the train and after giving my description of the man to the sheriff, found that he lived in Hazen. I caught another train to Hazen and walked two miles out into the woods where the man was logging. I told him I had to have the money or I would turn him over to the sheriff, so he got hold of his brother who gave me the money. I stayed all night in Lonoke, west of Carlisle, and took the train back to Little Rock the next morning.

I was 18 years of age on March 21, 1917 and was then a salesman in the men's clothing department at Blass'. I had been able to quit my paper route sometime earlier when America entered the First World War on April 6, 1917. On April 9th, three days after war was declared, I quit my job at Blass' and having always had a love for horses, went to enlist in the cavalry. But they were not taking enlistments for that branch of the service so I joined the infantry. We had gone to war and I felt my place was in the army.

Chapter V

In the Infantry: World War I

Having joined the army, I went home, left a note for mama and went back down to the place of enlistment and met up with Lee Lamonica. A little fellow of Italian descent from Pine Bluff, he enlisted the same day I joined the army and we walked out to Fort Logan H. Roots together, a distance of about 5 miles. Fort Logan H. Roots was an old army post on the north side of the Arkansas River. It had been there a long time and consisted of brick buildings including the barracks, officer's quarters, guard house, a parade ground and all the facilities necessary for a small army post.

That first night we got into a dice game. I had about two dollars and soon went broke. "That fellow sure did even-roll you last night," Lee said to me the next day. "What do you mean?" I asked. "Don't you know how to shoot dice?" he returned. "No," I answered, "I've never shot any dice."

"Well," he said, pulling a pair of dice from his pocket, "I'll show you something."

Lamonica then taught me how to control the dice, how to set the various combinations and how to "even-roll" the dice on a soft surface like a blanket spread on a canvas cot. Another shot called the "Hudson:" is used in controlling the dice on a surface like the soft dust in a company street or a smooth canvas cot. I got a pair of dice and started practicing, soon becoming an expert. This was not unusual — everybody was "handling" the dice if he could.

We stayed in these barracks only so long as it took us to clear a place for a tent camp further north on the army reservation. We cleared the campsite with axes and most of the old and new soldiers suffered with blistered hands and sore muscles. But I was in good condition and it didn't bother me. Just as soon as we got the land cleared, which took several weeks, tents were erected and the whole regiment, the 153rd Infantry, moved into camp. There were about 1200 men at that time.

I was in Company "E." The company captain was very hard on his men and we were not fed properly. For breakfast we generally got oatmeal and milk. This milk, called "bluejohn," had very little cream in it. After pouring it on the oatmeal, we would let the weevils come to the top and dip them off before we ate it, and it was always full of weevils. The noon meal usually consisted of a jam sandwich. At night we got a better meal but still nothing to brag about.

While stationed there, we would sometimes hike down to the Arkansas River, which was a good deal downhill from where we were located. Our packs consisted of everything we had, including all of our clothing, toilet articles, extra pair of shoes, two blankets and a "shelter half." When fastened together with the other "half" carried by another soldier, it made up what was called a "puptent." These little puptents were only about 3 feet high but were sufficient for two soldiers sleeping on the ground. The pack was in addition to an ammunition belt, canteen full of water, bayonet in a scabbard and a rifle.

We would spend the day on the sandbars in various kinds of training. Many times it would be very hot and on the march back to camp, quite a few soldiers just could not make it and would "fall out" from exhaustion. They would be picked up by headquarter's company wagons and hauled back to camp. Some of the soldiers, however, would fake exhaustion and usually picked a shady spot to "fall out." When one fell out in such a spot, he was told by a non-com to get his ass up from there and get going.

The captain formed what was called a "silent squad" which was made up of men the captain wanted to punish but who hadn't done anything bad enough to be sent to the guardhouse. The men in this squad were not allowed to speak to anyone and no one was allowed to speak to them. They were required to walk at attention at all times and, when one of them had to go to the latrine — and it didn't make any difference if it was two o'clock in the morning — they all had to go marching at attention.

These men had to do all the dirty work around the company area like cleaning the latrines. They were not allowed to write any letters, they were not allowed to smoke, and no one liked the corporal who was in charge of the squad. After a few months the captain was transferred and it was a fortunate thing for him that he was. If he had been sent to France with this group of men, it is likely he would not have lasted long. Someone would have shot him during the first fire exchange with the enemy.

Late in 1917, our division was sent to Camp Beauregard, Louisiana, for training. It was bitter cold, we were in tents, and the flu was epidemic. Many soldiers died and coffins were hauled out by the wagonload on a daily basis. Because of the flu we had to furl the tents each day and air everything out real good. One day our tent was furled up around a hot Sibley stove and a big hole was burned in one side of it. We never did get a new tent or even get that one repaired and it got down to zero and below on several occasions that winter.

Although the conditions were rough, men dying daily with the flu, inadequate shelters, sleeping cold every night with only two single blankets on a canvas cot, food that was not too good, long hikes carrying heavy packs, there was no complaining from the soldiers. We took all of it just as part of being a soldier.

Early the next spring, by which time I was a sergeant, the 39th Division including the 153rd Infantry went by train from Camp Beauregard, Louisiana, to Newport News, Virginia. There we would spend only a few days before boarding the Huron for France. With the exception of one man who claimed he was lame (though we thought he was faking), we were all anxious to go. One of the soldiers, a good friend of mine, had a bad case of gonorrhea. He had not reported to the hospital for treatment because he thought it would prevent him from going overseas. When it came time to board the Huron, he was in a weakened condition and in no shape to make the ten mile march from our camp to the ship. So I carried his 65 pound pack along with my own while two other soldiers helped him make the march. In this way he got aboard the ship and when we were well out to sea he reported for treatment. I don't know exactly what happened to him because after we got to France, I never saw him again.

The Huron was a small freighter captured from the Germans and converted to a troop ship. There were about twenty-five hundred of us on the ship and we all tried to stay on deck. It was stuffy down in the hold and it was evident to all of us that it was better to be on deck in the event the ship was torpedoed.

A portion of the hold not being used for cargo had been divided into compartments. They had been equipped with bunks three deep - one above the other - with about 60 men in each compartment. We reached our compartment in the hold by going down a ladder and in the event the ship was torpedoed, there would have been a terrible mess. All those still living would have been fighting to get up that ladder. Thus, it was really crowded with most of the soldiers sleeping on the wooden deck. I slept on a big coil of rope for the two weeks it took to cross the Atlantic to France. I claimed that spot as my own and would have fought to keep it.

The food was good. It came around in big vessels and was served to us in our mess kits wherever we happened to be. Being so crowded, there wasn't much room to maneuver, and it was easier to serve the food to the men than have the men come to the food.

We kept watch for submarines at all times from certain stations on the ship. There were a large number of ships in that convoy and it was surrounded by our torpedo boats, which is probably why we did not see an enemy submarine on the way over there. Most of us spent a good part of the time being seasick anyway.

We landed at Brest in France and everyone wanted to go to town immediately, but no one was allowed to leave the ship. The ship was tied to a dock and the deck of the ship was not very far above the floor of the dock. Some of us decided that if we were compelled to stay on the ship the next day, we would just jump down onto the dock and slip off uptown.

But the ship had a cargo of oats as well as soldiers. The cranes worked all night unloading the oats and the next morning the deck of the ship was so high above the dock, that it was impractical to jump down with any degree of safety. But that day we were moved off ship and marched through Brest on out to the adjoining countryside.

We made bivouac in a turnip patch and our company was in a spot surrounded by a dirt fence which reminded me of a small version of the levees back home. That afternoon a big truck came in loaded with quarters of beef which were unloaded in a pile on the ground. Another soldier and I managed to get hold of a hindquarter and carried it to our company and built a fire. Everybody was free to help themselves and so men cut off pieces of meat to suit themselves and cooked it over the open fire. We all ate for the biggest part of the night.

We did not stay at Brest very long, but while we were there, some of us made it downtown a couple of times. There was an old church, perhaps several hundred years old, and on top of the outside walls there were statues about three feet high at approximately eight-foot intervals all the way around the church. We were told that the statues were carved by members of the congregation who would work at home and bring them to the church when completed.

There was one statue that was very pornographic and the story I heard was that it was carved by a young man who had been reprimanded by the church and was very angry about it. He placed the finished statue on top of the wall behind some temporary scaffolding. The statue was not recognized for what it was until after the church had been dedicated and therefore, could not be changed. I do not know the validity of the story, but I did see the statue. And in all probability it is still there.

We were shipped out of Brest in French boxcars which were very small compared to American boxcars. Printed on all of them was "Quarante hommes ou huit cheveaux," in English, "Forty men or eight horses," - and forty men in one of those little boxcars made it so very crowded that you could not lie down to sleep. There was only room to sit on the floor and we were all jammed very close.

We pulled into a railroad yard at some good-sized city and were put on a siding. Our car was at the end of the train and five or six of us saw an empty boxcar sitting on the siding behind our car. We just pushed the empty car up to our car and coupled them up. This was very easy as the coupling was just a link, not like the couplings on American trains.

We took possession of the car and when the train pulled out, we had plenty of room. It was very cold, but we managed to get some firewood at the next stop and we built a fire on the floor of the boxcar. It wasn't very long until the floor of the car was burning, so we moved the fire to another spot and put out the burning floor. This was not hard to do as there were no toilets in the boxcars. We eventually burned almost all of the floor in the boxcar, but we were pretty comfortable as long as it lasted.

We were shipped to the little town of Ruilly, located in a wine-growing district of France. We were billeted in a school from which all the furniture had been removed and all the desks were stacked up against a high rock wall at the back of the school yard.

There was a town water pump a short distance from the school, but the women of the town would go down to a little river to wash their clothes. And they washed them differently than I have ever seen. The women placed the clothes on rocks at the river's edge and pounded them with wooden paddles. Evidently that got the clothes clean.

There was plenty of wine to be had and, on occasion, I had my share, but there was very little drunkenness among the men. The French were not not allowed to sell cognac to American soldiers although there was a copper still down by the river. The cognac was made just about the same way corn liquor is made here, but I believe the cognac is made using the residue left from making wine.

There was a small slaughterhouse nearby and we bought meat there when they would let us have it. They used a method for skinning a calf I have never seen anywhere else. After the calf was killed and hung up, it was bled with every drop of the blood being saved. The man, who operated the slaughterhouse by himself, inserted a rubber hose in a small hole in the skin of the calf. He then used a hand air pump to force the skin away from the flesh making it easy to remove the hide.

While there I kind of took up with a girl about my age who lived in a house right back of the school. I could climb up the pile of school desks, go over the top of the wall, and drop down in her yard. Her parents were friendly to me and they always had French bread with butter and jam — that French bread just could not be beat.

Our company stayed there quite a while, but we were finally shipped to another little town where, for the most part, we were billeted in the attics of houses. Instead of going through the homes to get to the attics, we climbed ladders on the outside entering through dormer windows.

As I said before, the French were not allowed to sell us cognac. But one day a friend, Albert Shields, and I asked a girl on the street if she could get us some. She said to come to her house that night, which we did and knocked on the Dutch door of her small home. She led us into a room that was a pretty good size. It had a fireplace and there were two old ladies in the room sitting on opposite sides of the fireplace. One was a good deal older than the other. There were also a couple of beds in the room occupied by sleeping children. Two chairs were pulled up in front of the fireplace for us. We gave the girl, who was about eighteen years old, some money and she went after the cognac.

While she was gone I got to talking to the younger of the two ladies. I had learned just enough French by that time to carry on limited conversations. The old lady asked me if there was much flu in the American army and I said there was some. She then said, "Grandma over there and all the kids have the flu." When the girl got back with the cognac, my friend and I took it and left immediately.

We decided there was a good chance of us taking the flu, having been in a room with so much of it. So we tried to kill all the flu germs with the cognac. I wasn't used to drinking and

Shields and I got drunk as skunks and had some difficulty getting up the ladder to our attic, but we finally made it. After I laid down, the room went round and round for quite a while.

Our division never did go to the front as a unit while I was with it, but some of the men were sent up as replacements from time to time. One day we were told that a platoon of men and two sergeants were to go to the front. There were twelve sergeants in the company and, when the captain asked for volunteers, all twelve of us stepped forward. We drew straws to see who would go and I got one of the two short ones. But that night the captain said that orders had come from headquarters as to which sergeants were to go with the platoon and that I was not one of them. I have always had my doubts about those orders as those who went never came back. This was winning against the odds!

A short time later I was told that I had been selected to go to an Officer's Candidate School and that the next morning I was to be at the railway station in another little town about four miles away. I got up early and walked to the station. There were other soldiers there from the division who had also been selected to attend the school.

But I soon discovered that I had left my billfold under my pillow in my billet, and I had the equivalent of about eight dollars in my wallet. I learned that it would be about 3 hours before the arrival of the train, so I ran back to the attic, got my wallet and ran back to the station — a distance of about eight miles, though that was no big deal for me at the time.

The candidates for Officers School were taken across France in the boxcars to the city of Langres and the school was held at an old French fort, Fort Conulo. I was not confronted with any problems in the school although many others had trouble with map making. But I already knew almost everything that was taught by virtue of having gone through an S & S (Sergeant & Subaltern) School at Camp Beauregard.

The only problem was that we ran out of food due to transportation difficulties, and for a period of about two weeks, all 250 of us had practically nothing to eat except carrots. The cooks fixed them in every possible way to cook a carrot but it was a long time after the war before I would eat one again.

While at the Officers Training School, I met John Edwards. He was from Arkansas but we were not from the same outfit. John and I became close friends. He was tall, dark and handsome, intelligent and was good company. Years later, John became president of a bank at Batesville, Arkansas, and helped me when I ran for the Supreme Court.

On one occasion while at the Officers Training School, John and I were just prowling around the countryside and ran across a farmhouse. We got into a conversation with the farmer and his wife and made arrangements with the wife to fix us a good dinner a few days in the future. The lady said she had everything including the chicken but was short on flour and so we were to bring the bread. When the time came around, we obtained passes and went to town and managed to buy a large loaf of French bread. We started walking to the farmhouse out in the country, a distance of about three miles. We hadn't gone far when a U.S. Army truck came by going in the same direction. It slowed up for something and John, who was carrying the bread, and I were able to get in the back of it. But when we got to where we had to get off, the truck was going pretty fast. I got down first, lowering myself to the ground and running as fast as I could while hanging from the back of the truck, but managing to stay on my feet when I finally let go. Then John got down and turned somersaults. I could not see him very well in the dark and my chief concern was what happened to the bread! I ran to him hollering out, "Du pain! du pain!" (the bread! the bread!). Later in life John kidded me about this, but the bread was only slightly damaged and we went on to the farmhouse where we had a big, excellent meal and the cost was very little.

At the officers school, each of us was given a large notebook and told to make notes on the things we heard in lectures. I soon learned that I could not listen like I wanted and write notes at the same time. So I didn't take notes of any consequence. After a few weeks we were told that there would be an examination and that all those who passed would get their commission.

The test, which was given in the messhall, was a written one and we were to place our notebooks on the table while we were taking the test. A major came down the aisles looking at everyone's notes. He picked up my notebook and seeing all the blank pages, threw it back on the table asking where my notebook was. I told him I had just finished one and this was the second one. I don't know what I would have done if he had ordered me to go get the first one. I might have just kept on going. But he didn't, and I was one of the sixty men in the class of two hundred and fifty to pass the examination.

Papers had to be filled out whereby we would be discharged as soldiers and taken back in the army as commissioned officers. These papers were all completed but on that very date, November 11, 1918, the Armistice was signed and, with no need for more officers, our commissions were withheld. At a later date however, I did get a commission in the reserve corps signed by General Pershing which I still have and value highly. I was nineteen years old at the time.

A few days after the Armistice was signed, those of us who had passed the examination were shipped out. We did not know where we were going but again took to the boxcars, the "forties and eights," at Langres and headed somewhere. That night we stopped at a good-sized city, Tours or Dijon, as I remember.

We were cold and hungry, having had nothing to eat that day. By inquiring around, another soldier and I found a Salvation Army hut about two blocks away. We went there immediately to get some coffee and donuts. I think the Salvation Army is the best organization of its kind in the whole world. They always helped us in any way they could while we were in France and they would never take a dime.

When we got back to the railroad yard our train had pulled out taking our packs, duffle bags and rifles with it. We had no idea where the train went and we also had no idea where we were, so we just hung around the yard and waited for another train going in the same direction. In a fairly short time one came by. It was a freight train but we couldn't find a car we could get in, so we asked the engineer if we could ride in the cab with him and he allowed us to do so.

The next day we pulled into LeMans and learned that our outfit was located at some old French barracks nearby. When we went there, we found a large wall around the whole place and the guards would not let us enter because we had no papers. We went back into LeMans and got a room at a hotel. We had some money from being paid off at the school and stayed at the hotel for several days and really had a big time. When we tried to rejoin our outfit again, we managed to get in but we never did recover our belongings. It didn't make any difference, though, the war was over.

The war was over! There wasn't much discipline and everybody was doing just about whatever he wanted. We were put in with a lot of other soldiers who had also been separated from their outfits to form the 1206th Casual Company.

The war was over and everybody wanted to go home, but we didn't get to do this for quite a while. In fact, it was five months later, the following April, before we set sail for America. In the meantime we did just about whatever we wanted. Drilling was not required and everything was pretty loose.

One time John and I went to Paris but had no passes. We just got on a passenger train that was going there. The French passenger coaches had an aisle down the side and there were little compartments, each with room for about six people. Edwards and I walked down the aisle of one of these coaches until we found a compartment that wasn't full. There just happened to be a very pretty girl in there, about twenty years old. We sat down and soon began to talk to the girl who didn't pay any attention to us although we had some very complimentary things to say about her — in English, of course.

In a little while at another stop, the conductor came by to collect the tickets. "Votre billet, s'il vous plait," he said. We made out like we didn't understand. "Nous ne comprons pas," we responded. The girl spoke up in perfect English and told us the conductor would not allow us to ride in this compartment unless we had tickets. And, she added, we were on a first-class coach. We made a hasty exit, got off the train, just walked back to a third-class coach and got back on. No one disturbed us there and we went on to Paris.

As we pulled into Paris we realized we could not go out the front doors of the station because there were Military Police who would pick us up. We jumped off the train before it reached its platform and took a roundabout way to the front of the station where we found a subway going uptown. We got on and asked which stop would put us in the main part of Paris. We were told to get off at Madelaine Church and I believe we were on Italian Boulevard when we got off the subway. We walked up the street in the direction where it appeared the action was.

We met quite a few girls who wanted us to go with them. The raincoats we were wearing had a shawl effect on the back and there were ventilation holes in the material underneath the shawl. They all seemed to be familiar with the construction of the raincoats and ran their hands up under the shawl sticking the fingers in the holes.

We passed up the girls until we met two very pretty ones. They looked a whole lot above average but they wouldn't pay any attention to us. So we fell in step and started talking to them. They finally came around. The upshot of it was that the four of us went to the Folies Bergere and then to dinner at a really good restaurant there on Italian Boulevard. It was the swankiest restaurant I had ever seen. Everything was the best, including the dress of the waiters.

I had been in a dice game and had won about twelve hundred francs and Edwards was well-heeled too. We let the girls order, telling them to order the best, and we enjoyed dinner very much. When the waiter brought the bill, the girl I was with insisted on checking it off against the menu. She cut the bill by half. We had indeed been overcharged but, in the end, it wasn't too expensive.

Edwards and I stayed in Paris for several days and had rooms at a very nice hotel. The girls took us on tours of the city and we saw a great deal of the area and, for some reason, I was especially fascinated with the Palace of Justice.

To get back to camp at LeMans, we had to go through the front of the railway station. The MP's stopped us and asked for our passes. We told them we were lost and had wound up in Paris. We said we knew where we were supposed to be, we just didn't know how to get there. They let us go saying it was mighty funny that every time a soldier got lost in France, the only place he could find was Paris!

The camp at LeMans was an old French army facility about two square blocks in area. It had barracks constructed of wood and was surrounded by a high rock wall. The bathing facilities were extremely limited. There were about fifteen thousand soldiers in that small area and the only way you could get a bath was to show that you had "cooties," as body lice were called. If you couldn't find a "cootie" on yourself, you borrowed one from a fellow who had plenty of them. You held it between your fingers in your undershirt while you waited in line, then showed it to the one on "cootie duty" and got a bath.

The 1206th Casual Company stayed at LeMans that winter, a pretty good-sized town that had a lot of girls. In March we were shipped to Brest in the "forties and eights," of course. We stayed in Brest until sometime in April and then boarded the battleship "Michigan" for the journey home. The ship was huge and our company, all two hundred and fifty of us, were the only soldiers aboard. The food was real good as we were fed the same as the sailors. It was of the best and there was plenty of it. The ship was not at all crowded and I enjoyed the trip. The North Atlantic had some real rough seas, but the big battleship just plowed through the waves. I had learned on the trip over that if you stayed near the center of the ship, there was not nearly as much movement and I never did get seasick. Sometimes I went up on the very top deck (I think it is called the boat deck) and watched the waves breaking over the bow of the ship.

During the trip I had a little tough luck. I got into a blackjack game and, in the course of the game, I got the deal. After dealing a while, I broke myself in two hands running without breaking anybody else and had to pay off everybody in the game. I just borrowed a few dollars, got into a dice game and won most of it back.

After an eleven-day trip we landed at Newport News, Virginia, stayed there a few days, and then I was given a train ticket to Camp Robinson, Arkansas. Shortly after arriving there I was discharged, given the pay I was due and a sixty-dollar bonus. This gave me enough money to buy some civilian clothes and I immediately went back to my old job as a salesman in the men's clothing department at Blass'.

I worked at Blass' for about two months before concluding it was not for me. I did not like the inside work and after being in the army, it was just too tame. It was three months past my twentieth birthday and I decided to go back to Lake Village. I did not know what I would do, but I was confident I could find some kind of work.

Chapter VI

Readland Plantation

One of the first people I met at Lake Village was George Cracraft who owned Readland Plantation. The plantation adjoined the little town of Readland about twenty-five miles south of Lake Village on Grand Lake, another of the river-made lakes. I had never met George before, but I knew who he was because my Aunt Brooksie, then about sixty years of age, was keeping house for him at Readland. And he knew who I was because Captain Cracraft, his father, and my Grandpa Robinson had been law partners at one time. George was in his late twenties and invited me to go home with him to visit my Aunt and I accepted.

Captain Cracraft had died quite a few years previously, leaving Readland to George's mother. She was much younger than her husband who had been about fifty when they married. George had bought out his sister's interest after their mother died.

There were two other white men working at Readland: Ivy Lasley, the head man under George, and a Mr. Emery, a riding boss. A riding boss is called that because he rides a horse in overseeing the work done by the dayhands, as the laborers are called. Mr. Lasley oversaw the entire operation of the plantation. Actually, George very seldom went over the place. He had not been educated with operating a plantation in mind. As a child he was sent away to school in the North, and then he went to college, and to Harvard Law School. At the time I went to work there, George was not practicing law, but later he did open a law office in Eudora.

Jack Chambers owned Lake Port Plantation located about fifteen miles north of Readland. After I was at Readland a few days, he and George bought about a hundred head of cattle at Portland, fifteen miles west of George's place. George asked me if I wanted a job and, of course, this kind of job is what I had wanted all of my life. He also hired Roy Matthews, a fellow about my age from Eudora, and he and Mr. Lasley and I went after the cattle. We rode across Beouf River Swamp and stayed in Portland that night.

Beouf River Swamp was a large area through which flowed the Beouf River, a slow moving stream that came from the north and drained thousands of acres of land. It was really more of a bayou than a river. I don't know what was the exact size of the area called the Beouf River Swamp, but I have an idea that it was about ten miles from east to west, and about twenty miles from north to south.

The swamp was an area from which most of the good timber had been removed but the drainage situation was such that it could not be farmed. It was too wet. But there were high places and ridges in the swamp that were well drained, and by taking advantage of these high places, there was a trail all the way across the swamp from east to west. In the dry season of the year, a person could ride horseback just about anywhere in the swamp. In other seasons, the ground stayed wet and in many places it was very boggy - a wet, muddy place where an animal would sink, having a hard time getting out and sometimes dying there.

There was a lot of wild game. Deer hunting was good and there were wild hogs which descended from tame hogs. A lot of cattle and hogs were turned into that area by people living nearby as there was no charge for anyone running stock there.

The next morning we took delivery of the cattle and headed back across the swamp. A cow would occasionally break away but it was easy to get it back into the herd, except when Roy rode out to turn one cow back and his horse bogged down to his belly. Roy climbed onto a tree limb and hollered for me to come get him while his horse struggled in the muck back to the trail. But I told him to just come on out by himself because my horse would bog down too. I threw him a rope, pulled him out and we got home with the cattle okay. The next day Chambers came with some of his men, separated out his cattle, and drove them on home. We put George's cattle with other stock that he already owned.

Readland Plantation is located on Mississippi River delta land, land built up from the river depositing silt during flood times. It is good alluvial soil. The whole plantation consisted of about twenty-five hundred acres: the eight-hundred-acre Home Place where we all lived and kept most of the equipment; the seven hundred acres north of Eudora; four hundred acres on the other side of Grand Lake; and four hundred acres a little further south.

George had a concrete silo on the Home Place that held fifty-five tons of silage, and another that held fifty tons on the land north of Eudora. In addition to feeding the livestock several thousand bales of hay that winter, I emptied both those silos with a fork. During that time Mr. Emery quit and after we put the cattle on pasture that spring, I was given his job as riding boss.

There were cabins scattered over the plantation, located at places convenient to the land that the occupant worked. They were all of the same type cabin, but there were two sizes: A small two-room cabin and a larger four-room cabin. The two-room cabin consisted of a fairly good-sized room about 16 X 16 in front, and a smaller room about 12 X 16 to the rear. There was a porch about eight feet wide across the front of the house and the roof of the house also covered the porch. The roof was rather steep, making a pretty good-sized attic which helped keep the house cool in the summer time. The sills of the house, the foundation timbers, rested on cypress blocks. These blocks were cut from cypress trees growing at various places in the water along the shore of Grand Lake.

A four-room cabin was built the same way, only there were two rooms in front, side by side,and two in the rear. Sometimes the rooms were divided in the middle by a hallway going from front to back. This hallway was called a "dog trot".

There was no running water. The water supply was from a hand-operated pitcher pump, one at each house, located in convenient places. We drove these pumps with a small hand-operated pile driver made of a heavy wooden block contained in a frame with the block and tackle at the top. It would be pulled to the top by hand and let fall on the two inch pipe that was being driven into the ground. This pipe was in about four foot joints and the first joint was a point. It was sharpened at one end and perforated by many small holes around which was a copper screen. The water entered these holes into the pipe and the screen kept out foreign matter.

At the back of the place, the water level was only about thirty feet deep. But at the front of the place, the level was about seventy-five feet deep. At one occasion, we were driving a pump at the front of the place and got into trouble at the seventy foot level. For some reason we were not able to drive the pump any further. We pulled it to try and see what the trouble was and embedded in the screen around the pump point there were pieces of cypress. We had driven into a cypress log seventy feet under the ground, showing that over a long period of time, perhaps centuries, the river had deposited its silt to at least that depth and no telling how much deeper.

Readland was operated like all other plantations in the delta country, each plantation having its own gin. A cotton plant is a bushlike stalk that produces "bolls" of cotton. A white cotton fibre matures in these round "bolls" about the size of a golf ball. These "bolls," which are in sections, open up when the cotton matures. Each "boll" contains many seeds to which are adhered the cotton fibre. This material, cotton and cotton seed, was picked out of the "bolls" by hand. Later this was done by machinery. A cotton gin removed the fibre from the cotton seeds and the fibre was put into large bales weighing about 500 pounds each. They were then shipped, usually to a cotton compress where they were pressed into smaller bales to facilitate shipping to its final destination, a large part of it to countries all over the world.

When it was discovered that the soil and the climate of the south were especially good for the production of cotton, there were no gins. And in the beginning of cotton production in the south and for a long time thereafter, the cotton fibre was removed from the seed by hand. Thus there was a need for much labor as this method was very slow. In the year 1793, Eli Whitney invented the cotton gin. This is a method of removing the cotton fibre from the seed very rapidly with large machinery in a large building, the average gin house being about 40 feet by 60 feet. The gins were powered by wood burning steam boilers and a crew of men from the plantation operated them, the same gin crews being used year after year. Due to their lack of experience with machinery, it is really remarkable that fieldhands handled this somewhat complicated machinery in a very efficient manner.

The Negroes did all the labor and there were several different classes of workers. The "dayhands" were mostly unmarried young men who boarded with families on the place. They did all kinds of work that came up and worked strictly by the day. There was quite a bit of acreage planted in the "day crops," cotton and corn, that was worked by day labor.

Then there were the "halfhands," the married couples, most of them having children. The couple was given enough acreage to plant cotton. This took up most of their time, but not all of it. They had some time to work as day labor and they were paid in cash each Saturday for the day work they had done that week. In addition to the land and a house to live in, the "halfhands" were furnished with the mules and equipment necessary to work the crop as well as a place to get wood for their fuel. They were given credit at the commissary for food and clothing, any medicine that might be needed, and the services of a doctor. The couple got half the money from the crop they had worked; the other half went to the plantation owner. The debt incurred at the commissary throughout the year was taken out of the couple's half of their money. There was usually some money left after the cotton was ginned and sold and this, along with the day labor money, made for a good arrangement.

A "sharecropper" had his own mules and equipment and the plantation owner furnished the land and credit at the commissary for the "sharecroppers'" needs throughout the year. He got three-quarters of what he produced and one-quarter went to the plantation owner.

The arrangement was about as good as could be made for everyone and was a way of life for both, whites and Negroes. The

Negroes had some money from day work, getting the necessities on credit at the commissary. The fact that the debt might never be paid off made no difference — they had nothing to lose. Meanwhile, the whites lived beyond their means on credit too.

Plantation owners were usually heavy in debt, but the enhancement of property values kept them going for a long time. Most wound up losing their plantations and the Great Depression of the 1930's wiped out just about everybody.

After 1940, plantation life as known prior to that time, became a thing of the past. Tractors and the implements used with them had come into their own and a large labor force was no longer needed to work cotton crops. In addition, fertilizers and pesticides were being developed. Soybean crops, now widespread in the South, were beginning to appear and needed no hand labor. These things, combined with the need for factory laborers in the Second World War, led to the migration of the Negroes to the cities of the North.

There were many enjoyable hours on George Cracraft's Readland Plantation. The relationship between whites (there were four of us) and Negroes on Readland was good. We respected each other. I talked a great deal to some of the elderly Negroes and they taught me a lot. One was Uncle Jim Jefferson. "Uncle" was just a term of respect and nothing else. Just why some elderly Negroes were called "Uncle" or "Aunt" and others were not, I do not know. The cook at the big house at Readland, the main residence, was called Aunt Mary. Her husband, who also worked at the big house, was not called Uncle Bob even though he was just as old and was just as good as Aunt Mary. And there was Louis Hester, just as old and good as Uncle Jim Jefferson, and he was not called Uncle Louis.

I spent considerable time talking to Louis while he was chopping the grass and weeds out of the cotton with a hoe. He used an old-time hoe, one of his own and much heavier than the ones in common use at the time, but also more effective. Louis had several children. The oldest was Hattie, who was in her early twenties and had recently married a man named Josh Shinehouse on the place. In one of our long talks Louis remarked that he was glad Hattie had married. I said, "I don't see why, Louis, she is a good hand and always helped you make a good crop." Louis replied, "Well, she's a breedin'uhman," adding that she had four children before she got married and that he just wasn't able to feed all those kids.

Many words were pronounced by the southern Negro in a manner all their own and it was not altogether mispronunciation. It was simply their way of saying the word, like: "uhman" for "woman" and "gwine" for "going." It cannot be said that "gwine" is a mispronunciation of "going," it was simply one of their words.

"Vittles" was a word frequently used by Negroes instead of "food." It is in the dictionary and derived from "victuals," but I have never heard a white person use the word. And, "seed" took the place of "have seen."

Saturday night was a real social event for most people, but especially for the Negroes. I remember one saying to the effect, "If a white man was a 'nigger' just one Saturday night, he'd never want to be a white man again."

Joe Green and John Jefferson were two of the Negro boys at Readland and both of them were about sixteen years old when I was there. And there was an older Negro girl, Gistine, who was about twenty-two or twenty-three years old. After I left Readland, I heard nothing of them for about forty years. Then one day the phone rang and it was Joe Green. We had a good long talk and he told me he had been a preacher for many years. I asked about John Jefferson and Joe said, "Gistine kilt 'im." The two were going together, got into a quarrel and, as Joe put it, "Gistine stabbed 'im." Several years later I tried to find Joe to visit with him but he had moved and I could not locate him.

The southern Negro had a good sense of humor. They would pull pranks on one another and pass along the latest joke. One joke I still remember went something like this:

> The boss man sent a little nigger boy down to the lake to get a bucket of drinking water for some plowhands nearby. The little boy came back immediately and said, "I seed an allygater and I'se skeered!" The boss man told him to go

> back and get the water, that the alligator was just as scared of him as he was of the alligator. The little boy replied, Cap'n, if dat allygater iz haf as skeered of me as I iz if it, dat water ain't fittin' to drink!

There were several months during the year when we didn't have much to do. But when we did work, we worked long hours, daylight to dark, fifteen hours a day or more, usually five days a week. At one time I had about thirty women hoe-hands chopping cotton. The wages were sixty cents a day. There was one man, crippled in one leg, who stayed with the women hoe-hands and kept their hoes sharpened. When one of the cotton choppers fell behind with her row, he also helped her catch up. One day Hattie Shinehouse kept on falling behind and I spoke to her about it. It was about three in the afternoon on a real hot July day — you could see "heat monkeys" rising from the cotton. This happened when there was moisture in the soil and the sun was real hot. Hattie looked up at me and said, "Lord, Mr. Sam, it's worth sixty cents a day just to be out here." "I guess you're right," I replied and rode on.

Ida, a big stout woman, carried the lead row. She set the pace and the other hoe-hands were supposed to keep up with her and for this she was paid seventy-five cents a day. This doesn't seem to be very much, but on the other hand, as riding boss I made forty dollars a month plus room and board. And I worked from daylight to dark while the hoe-hands didn't come to work until an hour after sunrise and quit an hour before sundown. I also worked on Saturdays in the commissary, issuing rations to the Negroes who came there to get their supplies. They would put on their best clothes that day and there was a lot of visiting. Many of them would hang around all day as there was a porch on the front of the commissary with benches to sit on.

There were public schools for their children to attend, and the health of the people on the place was good. During the time I was at Readland there was only one death on the place and that was Uncle Jim Jefferson, and I believe he was killed by a doctor giving him too much "Calomel." "Calomel and quinine" was the remedy for everything back then. Quinine is to cure malaria. I don't know just what calomel is supposed to do, but it was given to just about anybody who got sick. We all went to Uncle Jim Jefferson's funeral. He was buried there on the place in a small cemetery.

I do not remember one person, man, woman or child, ever being sick on the place except Uncle Jim Jefferson and me. We kept "Black Draught" in the commissary and sometimes someone would get a package of it. It was some kind of medicine but I never did know what it was supposed to do. I think it was a purgative, but I'm not sure.

One time when George Cracraft and his wife had gone away somewhere, I became so ill that I felt I should go to the hospital. I had a very high fever and felt sick all over. I knew it was malaria. There was one Negro on the place who knew how to drive an automobile and he drove me to Dr. MaGee's hospital in Lake Village. That night the doctor gave me 40 grains of quinine with a hypodermic needle about two inches long in my right buttocks. It was one of the most painful things I ever experienced. The next night the same thing was repeated in the other buttocks. The next day I decided I would not suffer that pain again and left the hospital. But they told me to take 10 grains of quinine a day for 60 days. I did this and was never again bothered with malaria.

One day during the noon hour, a group of hoe-hands were resting under a big pecan tree near the barn. Ida, a big stout woman who "carried the lead row," complained of not feeling good. I went to the barn and got a capsule that we had there for the mules. It was about one half inch in diameter and about two inches long, the biggest capsule that was ever made. I handed it to Ida and everybody, including Ida, just about died laughing. She made no more complaints about not feeling good. Of course, if she had really been sick, I would not have pulled this stunt.

All the plantations in the delta country of Arkansas, Louisiana and Mississippi were operated pretty well the same way. The white people lived a good life and the Negroes, not knowing any other life, were satisfied with their conditions.

Actually, by today's standards the living conditions were very bad. In fact, "awful" would be a more accurate description. Slave traders had bought slaves in Africa, often from the chiefs of the tribes and frequently from the kinfolk of the very slaves being sold. They were then brought to this country and sold in slave markets as slavery was entirely acceptable at that time. Some centuries later at the end of the Civil War, their freedom did not amount to much. The United States government did nothing for them except that President Lincoln issued a proclamation that they were free. But they had nothing; no land, no home of their own and no skills except the knowledge of how to raise cotton. Their former owners also had nothing except debts and heavily mortgaged ground. In many instances all improvements including the dwelling houses had been burned, and the Confederate money was completely worthless.

In these conditions, the problem for both the whites and the Negroes was one of survival and they did the best they could. The white people eventually lost their plantations, though some held on for a long time due to the gradual enhancement in value of the land, and they were able to make new loans.

Practically all of the people of the southern states (as well as many others), were brainwashed into the belief that Negroes were inferior people - that they did not amount to much, this no doubt coming from the fact that at one time the Negroes were slaves and just personal property to be bought and sold.

Brainwashing is one of the most powerful forces on earth. Everybody is subject to being brainwashed, even those with the most brilliant minds. This is proven beyond a shadow of a doubt by the different religions of the world. One race of people including some of the smartest people on earth, have been brainwashed to believe in a certain religion and this belief cannot be shaken. Those having that belief will die defending it. On the other hand, other people, just as smart and with equal fervor, believe just as strongly in an entirely different religion and will die supporting their belief in that respect. They cannot all be right but they have been brainwashed into their beliefs. They did not come into the world believing anything. They were brainwashed into their beliefs, some valid and some invalid. And the same thing applies in many other areas. When one is taught to strongly believe something that is not true, he is brainwashed.

Southern white people believed that any treatment of a Negro as a social equal, was a downright disgrace and it was therefore not done. This belief was as strong as a religious person's belief in his religion. I never heard of a Negro being asked to dinner in a southern home. The white people of the Delta liked Negroes (this cannot be said of the "hill" people) and would go a long way to help them, especially the ones they knew personally. They would make personal sacrifices for them, even on occasion risking their lives for them. But to treat one as an equal socially, it simply was not done. In fact, this brainwashing extended to the Negroes themselves. With few exceptions, they did not believe that they were as "good" as the whites. Of course, now the Negroes have freed themselves from such brainwashed beliefs and the whites are on the way. But that brainwashed condition still exists to a large extent in the South.

I have said that the conditions in which the Negro lived were very bad. And they were, although at that time in the early 1920's it was not considered as such by either the white people or the Negro. As a matter of fact, no thought was given to it at all. But now I know that those conditions could have been made better if some thought had been given to it. Actually, I was not in a position to have done much along that line, but I could have done more than I did. I deeply regret that I did not do so.

For instance, some of the houses in which the Negroes lived were old and not tightly constructed. They were cold in the winter, having for heat only a woodburning fireplace and they did not have enough wood to keep the place warm. Not having enough wood was the fault of the occupant because he had sufficient opportunity to get in a good wood supply but simply hadn't done it. Few of them ever did. They sometimes then used the steps and porches of the houses as firewood. We had to guard against this. I could have made them get in a wood supply. I just didn't give it a thought.

Likewise, the Negro families had every opportunity to raise a good garden which would have furnished them with a much better food supply than they normally had. But most of them did not raise a garden. I could have seen to it that they did make one. In fact, if I had it to do over, I would have provided for a community garden. Even though just a riding boss, I could have done this and I could have seen to the garden being worked and an abundance of vegetables raised for everybody on the place.

I could have encouraged them to raise some hogs and give themselves a better supply of meat. But I did not do so. I just never thought about it. I could have demanded that they make small, needed repairs on the houses in which they lived to make them more comfortable in cold weather. I could have talked in favor of having a better supply of warm clothing in the commissary. On occasion, I carried candy with me on my horse and gave it to little children on the place, who would line up when they saw me coming. I could have done more of this.

But life on Readland wasn't all bad for the Negroes. Saturday was payday and after visiting at the commissary all day, usually till it closed at ten at night, many of them went down to an empty house on the place and shot dice. There was a church also on the place and on Sundays many Negroes attended.

When we were working with the mules near our headquarters, we would go there at lunch time. Only a few minutes would be taken in eating lunch and frequently the hands would have a baseball game for the rest of the hour. I was in my early twenties and I would be one of the players. Most of the players were dayhands and in my age bracket. I did not lose their respect by playing with them. Not every white person could do that.

Most of the mules used on the plantation had names, but the names were seldom used by the Negroes, mostly it was just plain "mule." One of the exceptions was Josh Shinehouse who worked a mule named "Blue" most of the time. He always called her by name and he didn't want anybody else working "Blue." I am satisfied that there were days he came to work just to keep anyone else from working that mule.

On work days the hostler rang the plantation bell one hour before daylight and the hands got to the lot at headquarters where the mules were kept, caught them up, and were ready to go to the fields by sunup. There was the story of the Negro hand who got to the mule lot before daylight and catching up his mule said, "Whoooa, mule! Ah put you in here las' night n' I'se takin' you out las' night."

There was one sour note on the place and that was the hostler, a big bright mulatto with straight hair and regular features who looked more Indian than Negro. He was sullen, talked very little and his name was Clarence. All of the Negroes disliked him, including his half-brother who worked on the place and also looked like an Indian. But Clarence had ingratiated himself with George who did not recognize the hostler's true character. The man was just looking for trouble

One time when he was driving a wagon on a narrow dirt road along the lake bank, he ignored a car that had pulled in behind him and was honking to be let by. The car just happened to be driven by Calmese Merritt, the County Sheriff, who was a tough man and usually didn't take anything off anybody. But this time he let the hostler get by with his unreasonable conduct because he knew that Clarence was George Cracraft's "nigger."

Almost all the white men on plantations had some particular Negro that was their favorite and they didn't want anyone fooling around with him. Such a Negro was known in the community as that particular white man's "nigger."

Practically all of the Negroes at Readland were afraid of the hostler. He had two little girls, one about seven years old, the other two years younger and he took them with him on all occasions. Wherever he went, from his house to the lot, from the lot to the big house, or to the post office for the mail, he had the girls with him, one on each side. I think he did this so that, if he had any trouble with someone, the other person would hesitate to shoot because of the little girls.

He always carried a pistol and I got a glimpse of it several times. He wore a blue denim jacket over his overalls, even on the hottest days of summer, and I am sure the jacket was worn to hide his gun.

There was another Negro, Phil McGee, who was not afraid of the hostler. Phil was not a big man and was a little crippled in his back. He had been in the Mississippi penitentiary and was as tough as a boot. One day we were putting silage in the silo near the barn. Phil was one of the workers and the hostler came over near the silo. I was busy with the portable gasoline engine we were using and had my back turned when the trouble started. The first thing I knew, Phil was at the back door of his house, which was only about a hundred feet away, and was cursing the hostler with every name he could think of. Phil told Clarence to come on over there, he had just the medicine for him. The hostler didn't go and that was the end of the incident.

After I became riding boss, it was necessary that I give the hostler his daily orders, which he resented and I felt it. His resentment may have been due in part to the difference in our ages — I was not yet twenty-one and he was nearing forty. But I knew how George felt about him and I avoided any trouble although, on many occasions, I was sorely tempted to give him a piece of my mind.

The showdown came late one evening and, of course, he had his little girls with him. Part of his duties were to put out feed and water for the mules at the mule barn and for the saddle horses, which were kept in a lot close to the big house. Passing through the lot on my way to the house that evening, I noticed there was no feed put out for my horse. I felt the omission as deliberate, and I did not overlook the incident as I normally did.

The hostler was still at the mule lot and I hollered down there and asked, in no uncertain terms, why he hadn't fed my horse. He hollered back for me not to talk so smart and I told him that I would show him how smart I was. I knew he had his pistol and I went in the back door to get a gun, a double-barreled shotgun. If I let him get by with his impudence, I would have lost the respect of all the Negroes on the plantation and my usefulness would have been greatly impaired.

George was on the front porch and heard the exchange of words between us. When I went in the back door to get the gun, George came around the house and just what he said to the hostler, I'll never know. When I came back out, the hostler was gone and I never saw him again. A few days later his wife and children moved from the place. I don't know where they went. The incident was never discussed between George and me.

Chapter VII

Shoutin' Pussies & Logging Contracts

There were never any dull times on the plantation. Not long after I went to work at Readland, George married Jean Scott, a beautiful young lady from Helena, Arkansas. When she came to the place, she brought a lot of life and pleasure with her. They had two children, Katie and George, Jr. George, Jr. is presently a member of the Arkansas Court of Appeals.

And there was always something to do. I knew a girl that lived fourteen miles up the levee and sometimes I would ride up to see her. I had a real good horse and, even though I rode in a lope a good part of the way, it was near daylight when I got back, just in time to get ready for another workday.

Just a mile or so up the lake there was a pavilion built out over the water and dances were held there with people coming from as far as fifty miles away to hear and dance to the good music, usually that of Bud Scott and his Negro orchestra from Natchez. These Negroes really furnished good music. Sometimes there was a Negro orchestra from Memphis, but never a white orchestra.

Many Sundays I rode my horse to Eudora where I played chess at Ralph's Drugstore all day. I belonged to a chess club and we met at a member's house once a month. Once, when it was my turn, Jean Cracraft put on a chess party for me. She served refreshments and also provided a box of cigars with the brand name, "Travis Club." None of the fellows smoked cigars and the whole box was left. I usually smoked cigarettes, rolling my own with "Bull Durham" or "Old North State" smoking tobacco. Since the cigars were there, I started smoking them and by the time I had smoked the whole box, I liked cigars pretty good. The next time I was in Eudora, I decided to get a cigar. I went into the drugstore and asked for a "Travis Club." The clerk gave me one and, to my surprise, asked for fifteen cents. This was quite a bit in those days, especially when I could get forty cigarettes out of a five-cent pack of smoking tobacco. It was the last cigar I ever bought.

The area around Readland was excellent for hunting: Goose hunting in the oatfields and on the islands in the Mississippi; deer hunting back in Beouf River Swamp and up near Weaver's Bayou; and the quail hunting was wonderful all over.

Fielding Wilson was a friend of ours who, with his uncle, had just sold the plantation they owned in Louisiana. At the time, I had a room back of the commissary, as did Mr. Lasley. It was 16 X 16, sealed with boards and furnished with a woodburning stove, which furnished heat to both rooms. Each room had a dresser, wash stand with a pitcher and a bowl, a bed and some chairs.

One cold, dark and rainy night there was a knock on the door. It was Fielding. He had just come from Louisiana and he had two bird dogs with him. The dogs were in terrible condition, just about as poor as a dog ever gets. Fielding said that while he was moving, he had left the dogs with a man in Louisiana. The fellow was making moonshine and prohibition officers had gotten after him. He had to run and had left the dogs — they like to starved. Fielding said that if we would keep the dogs and get them back in shape, we could have our pick of the two. Mr. Lasley and I agreed to that proposition and Fielding stayed with us that night and left the next morning.

The dogs were healthy. They just needed something to eat and, being bird dogs, it didn't take very long to get them in shape. One of the dogs was named "Sport" and the other was "Buck." They were absolutely the best bird dogs I have ever seen. Mr. Lasley and I were both pretty good shots and, with quail in abundance, we hunted a great deal, especially in the winter after all the cotton was ginned and there was not much to do. There was no bird limit and we brought home about seventy-five or eighty birds just about every time we went out. Most of our hunting was done with one dog as Fielding had come back after one of the dogs and we had kept old "Sport."

Fielding moved to his new place, Sterling plantation, a few miles south of Readland and he was up at our place quite a bit. George and Jean liked to have company and there were usually visitors at the big house.

In the spring of the year there was a small wild edible green in the area that we had on the table quite often. I don't know where the name came from, but they were called "shoutin' pussies," but no one thought any more about the name than they did peacocks, fighting cocks, jackasses or anything else with that kind of name.

One spring day, some of George's friends were there from up north and Fielding was also there for dinner. Of course, the greens were on the menu. During dinner Fielding remarked that he sure did "like shoutin' pussies when they were young and tender." I was sure one of the northern visitors was going to faint.

Carneal Warfield's family owned a fine plantation along Grand Lake. The dwelling house on the Warfield Plantation was built with bricks made at the place of construction by slave labor in 1840. The house burned in 1958.

On one occasion, several of us decided to go over to Cracraft's island on a goose hunt. This small island was in the middle of the Mississippi River, which was more than a mile wide in that area. Carneal had a batteau about sixteen feet long with a one-cylinder outboard motor. (Outboard motors of that period were simple and rather crude.) We all met at the river about three o'clock on that cold February morning. There were six of us, including a Negro named Pitman, and the boat was really overloaded.

Amos Warfield, a cousin to Carneal, got the motor started and we got out into the river. We were about a half mile out going downstream in the dark with about three miles to go when the boat ran up on some driftwood, killing the motor. After we got loose, the motor was hard to start and someone suggested that it be primed. There was a can of gas in the boat so Amos took the sparkplug out of the vertical cylinder and poured some gasoline into it. In doing so, he spilled some on the motor and when he tried to crank it, it backfired and set the gas on fire.

There we were in the middle of the Mississippi River at three o'clock on a bitter February morning with the outboard motor on fire. But Amos had good presence of mind. He pulled off his brand new hunting coat, purchased just the day before, threw it on the engine and smothered the flames. The motor then started, we went on down to the island and had a good goose hunt. The return trip was uneventful. At one point during the day, however, Pitman said he could just hear the news; "Five white folks and one 'nigger' drowned in the Mississippi River."

Each year about the first part of August the cotton crops were "laid by," that is, they could no longer be worked as they had grown too big and would be damaged. There was nothing more that could be done until it was time to start the picking in a couple of months. So, I took three logging teams to the woods to haul out logs for logging contractors.

Each team consisted of six mules, an eight-wheel log wagon with the necessary chains and skid timbers and a driver. There was one swamper for three teams. The swamper cleared the way for the wagon to be driven alongside the logs to be loaded. I would take twenty mules, which included two extra ones, four men and three wagons — two were Lindsay wagons and the other a Hemingway. There was no practical difference in the wagons — they were just different makes.

There was a lot of virgin timber, mostly gum, in that country at that time and we would make a subcontract with a logging contractor who was moving out a tract of timber. We stayed in tents at his camp and ate at his kitchen, arranged as part of the contract. We worked from daylight to dark, eating breakfast a little before daylight and supper after dark. We made about thirty dollars per day per team, gross profit, and that was pretty good money for the times.

Sometimes we ran across a "figured" gum, dark with a beautiful grain and is used primarily for furniture. These logs were kept separate as they brought a much higher price. I don't think any wood is prettier than "figured gum." I doubt that there is any gum timber left in the entire country. There was also a black gum that just could not be split. Many of the eight-wheel log wagons had the wheels boxed in, covered on the inside and outside with this timber to keep mud out of the wheels. The timber was so tough, that it could stand up under this use.

The six mules were hitched to the wagon, two abreast in tandem. The driver rode the nigh wheel mule, the mule on the left of the two nearest the wagon. Only one line was used in driving the team and this jerkline went from the driver to the nigh lead mule. A stick, called the "ban stick," went from the hames on the collar on the nigh lead mule to the bits of the off lead mule. By jerking on the line and saying "gee" (pronounced "yea") the nigh lead mule goes to the right and, of course, the "ban stick" pushes the off lead mule over. The team in the middle, the swing team, and the wheelers follow naturally. It takes a good deal of skill to drive six mules hooked to an eight-wheel wagon through the woods with one line, then putting the wagon alongside the logs to be loaded.

It was virgin timber that was being cut and the logs were big. We would load them by placing heavy timbers, called skid timbers, on the side of the wagon nearest the logs to be loaded. The skid timbers went from the bolsters on the frame of the wagon to the ground, one to the front and one to the back. Chains were fastened to each end bolster and went down the skid timbers. The end and slack of each chain was placed as close as possible to the log to be loaded which was then rolled onto these "bed chains." The lead mules were used to roll the log onto the "bed chains," then the bed chains were fastened to a chain called a "cross haul," and the mules rolled the log up on to the bolsters.

Many of the logs were so heavy that two mules could not load them and a block-and-tackle was used to assist the team. And sometimes a log was so big, the swing team had to be unhooked and brought around to help. Occasionally a log was so big, only one could be loaded on the wagon, rather than the usual two or three that were cut from one tree. On one occasion we loaded a twelve foot gum log that scaled around two thousand feet.

After the mules were hooked back into place, the driver mounted his saddle on the nigh wheel mule, picked up the jerkline...and the moment of truth had arrived. The load of logs was heavy, really heavy, and in order to start the wagon rolling, all of the mules had to pull together. And they had to keep pulling together with no letup until they got out onto the logging road. Up to that point, the driver had to maneuver around trees and stumps, and hubbing a stump meant real trouble and a lot of delay.

We worked in the logging woods until the fall rains started. Then the ground got soft which meant no more logging that year. We would pack up our camp, load it onto the wagons and go home.

One year on the way home, we came to a big field. The mules of the lead wagon got scared by something and started to run. The driver stayed in his place riding the nigh wheel mule of the runaway team and, using the jerkline, pulled the leaders to the left in a big circle. He had them going in a circle until finally the off wheel mule fell and all the rest stopped. The mule was fine, but parts of our camp were scattered all over the field.

It was 1920 and we began hearing rumors. The Negroes on the place were telling us that outsiders, including a white man from Little Rock, were appearing at churches and urging Negroes on plantations to rise up against white people, to take over, so to speak. We didn't pay much attention to the stories at first, although there was a Negro church on Readland. But we kept on getting these reports week after week.

We had never thought of preparing for anything like this and there were very few firearms on the place. We were not apprehensive regarding the Negroes who lived there on the plantation. But there were many others in the town of Readland and the surrounding countryside with whom we had no contact and did not know their feelings. (The Negro school had several hundred students; while the white school had only six.)

George owned a pistol, Mr. Lasley owned a shotgun, and I had a pistol and a shotgun. That was all. We were in a poor position to defend ourselves in the event that violence occurred, such as was being talked about. The talk continued and George thought we had better have some rifles, so he ordered several. There wasn't any trouble in our community, but later at Elaine, Arkansas, up the river about a hundred miles, there was a bad race riot. Quite a few people were killed and it was necessary for the governor to call out the National Guard.

One of the rifles George ordered in case of a riot at Readland was a 250-3000 Savage. It was very accurate and I could really shoot with it — I had qualified as an expert rifleman in the army. One day a flock of Canadian honkers landed in an oatfield near where I had a plow gang going. I loped my horse to the house, got the Savage, and returned to the oatfield. I got in a ditch, crawled within about a hundred yards of the geese and killed one with the rifle. We finished plowing at that spot by noon and I returned to the house with the rifle and the goose tied to my saddle.

Standing there waiting for me was a United States prohibition agent and the Sheriff, Calmese Merritt, my Aunt Mattie's husband. Calmese said he and the agent were going over to Cracraft Island in the Mississippi River to raid a still. This was in the days of national prohibition, and he asked me to go with them. They had rifles and of course, I was to take my rifle. I knew what might happen and did not want to go, but I couldn't refuse Calmese.

A Negro named Coleman had a skiff and was one of the few who could row a boat in the mile-wide Mississippi to the island. The current was strong but Coleman was a fine oarsman and had taken Jim Hunter and me over to the island on goose hunting trips. Coleman's skiff was twelve to fourteen feet long and it had a hole about three inches in diameter in the bow of the boat above the waterline. It had been blown there with a twelve-gauge shotgun at close range. I don't know the details about how this happened, but when the prohibition agent saw the hole, he said he would not go to the island in that boat, so we did not go at all.

There was no drinking of alcoholic beverages on Readland Plantation. None of the white people drank except on occasion when I would go to a dance, I would take a drink out of somebody's bottle. But so far as I know, there was never a drop of liquor on Readland. I am sure that none of the Negroes drank. Not because anything was said against it, it was just not done. It was never even mentioned one way or the other. If any drinking had been going on, I would surely have known about it. I knew about everything else that was going on.

But about 1930, some eight years after I left there, I was down at the little town of Readland and I ran into Horace Whittaker, a very able and intelligent Negro that had been on Readland Plantation when I was there. Horace was still there. We had a long conversation and I could tell from what Horace said, that there was at that time a good deal of drinking of liquor among the Negroes and in fact, I came to the conclusion that Horace, himself, was making liquor. Conditions were entirely different. A big change had taken place in that short period of time. George Cracraft no longer owned the place and the old plantation life was never to be the same again.

Chapter VIII

An Unforgettable Day

The Mississippi River drains a huge part of the United States. Every year as the snow and the ice melt in the north and in the Rocky Mountains, the river down in the delta country gets out of its banks and pushes up against the levees which protect the adjacent land from being flooded. The Mississippi River levee is a huge embankment of earth dug from land between the levee and the river. The levee runs on both sides of the river from below New Orleans north through the states of Louisiana, Mississippi, Arkansas and on into Missouri. It is now about two hundred feet wide at the base, about thirty feet high, and twenty feet wide at the top.

Most sections of the levees have good gravel roads on the top and are maintained by the federal government through the Corps of Engineers. But back in the early 1920's, the levees were maintained by local levee districts, and they were not nearly as big, strong or capable of holding back the river as they are now. At that time, they were only about four feet wide on the top and much lower.

When the levee broke, it was terrible. Once the water started going over the levee, it would soon wash out a crevice several hundred yards wide and the river would pour through this gap. The whole delta country would be flooded all the way back to the hill country many miles away, and for hundreds of miles to the south. This happened when the Arkansas River levee broke in the great flood in 1927. You could get in a boat at Little Rock and go to the Gulf of Mexico without ever getting in a main stream. So, each year when the river got out of its banks, the levees were watched carefully for any weak spots which were then repaired immediately.

In the spring of 1922, the river got extremely high and from all reports was going to go over the levee at a place called "Gaines Landing." It was an unwritten law in that country that when a "levee break" was threatening, everybody did whatever they could to prevent such a catastrophe. At Readland we got together eighty-five Negroes and the Levee Board put me in charge of them.

The Negroes knew that they were expected to go and try to save the levee. They also knew that they would make more money than usual by doing so. About a hundred more came from Eudora with a white man from that area in charge of them. We all went up the river to Gaines Landing on a barge pushed by a towboat.

The government had sent in a huge boat for sleeping and eating called a "Quarter Boat." I suppose the "Quarter Boat" was called that because of its use. The Negroes slept in bunks in large rooms while the white men had individual cabins on the upper deck towards the bow of the boat. The government furnished both the food and a crew of government employees to cook it — it was the very best.

The "Quarter Boat" was tied to trees growing between the levee and the river beyond the bar pits, which were now flooded over by water many feet deep. We went back and forth to the levee in skiffs, a distance of about two hundred feet. The bar pits were places where the dirt had been removed to be used in building the levee. I have never heard these pits called anything except "bar pits," but I have heard they were originally called "borrow" pits because the dirt was borrowed from one place to be put in another, in this case, the levee. Another version is that the original levees were built with wheelbarrows and the pits got their name from that source.

When we first got to Gaines Landing, the river was right close to the top of the levee in several places. For some reason, for a distance of about a quarter of a mile, the levee was a little lower then the rest of the levee and that's where the trouble was. Once it started going over the top, it would not take long to wash out a big gap and there was some apprehension that the break might come near the Quarter Boat, which then would be washed through the levee itself.

We immediately began filling bags with dirt from the land side, placing the filled bags on top of the levee. Thousands of burlap bags, about 1 ft. X 2 ft. in size had been sent in either by the Levee Board or the government. One of the workers would hold this bag open while another worker, using a shovel which had also been sent in, would fill the bag with dirt from what was supposed to be the dry side of the levee. In this instance, however, he filled it with muck - wet earth dug out of the ground which was already partly covered with seep water. The man holding the bag would then twist the end together, put the bag on his shoulder and carry it to the top of the levee where other men stacking the bags, would put it in place in a manner to hold back the river water. It was a messy job. There was seep water everywhere and it wasn't very long until everybody was covered with mud.

The river kept on rising. We would get ahead of it during the day, but by the next morning the water would be near the top of the bags that had been placed there the day before. We also had to reinforce places where "boils" broke out. These are places where the river seeps under the levee and comes out on the land side in a manner called a "boil." We strengthened the area of a "boil" by laying down poles and placing sandbags on top of the poles. Another way was to build a wall of sandbags around the spot. The water would then have to rise several feet to get over the top of the bags and, in so doing, drop its silt which then choked off the "boil."

We had been there about ten days and our replacements were due. We had kept the river from coming over the levee and there had been no griping or complaining. In fact, there hadn't even been a cross word and everything had been running smoothly. We were all on top of the levee, which was then about four feet wide, about 185 men in all waiting for the barge bringing our replacements. I had everybody move up the levee so that when the barge landed and the new workers got off, there would be no confusion.

When the barge arrived, one of the deckhands threw off a line so it could be tied. The nearest man to the line was a big, stout Negro from Eudora just about my age but I had had no personal contact with him. I told him to grab the line and tie it to a tree down near the base of the levee. He just folded his arms, looked me right in the eye, and didn't move.

We were standing fairly close together and I drew back a four foot long hickory stick that I had been whittling on. I wasn't necessarily mad, I was just enforcing my order. But before I could hit him, he ran into me, knocked me down, and landed on top of me. I knew he would kill me if he could. I managed to pull my revolver from my belt, a single-action Colt .45, but he got his hands on it with his forefinger around the hammer so I couldn't cock it. I had my forefinger through the trigger guard and he couldn't take the gun away from me as we struggled on top of the levee for possession of it. In a little bit I started to get the best of him and he begged me not to kill him. I told him to grab that line and tie that barge. He turned loose from the revolver and ran down the side of the levee, doing what he ought to have done in the first place.

In the meantime a Readland Negro, George Brown, saw what was happening from where he was at the far end of the line and was coming to my aid as rapidly as possible. He had a long switchblade knife in his hands and would have killed that other Negro had things not turned out as they did. The other white man was there and had a revolver in his pocket, but he never moved. I never spoke to him again.

At this point in time, 66 years or three generations later, my action on this occasion may not be understandable by most people. But I did what I did without giving it a thought. I did the only thing that could be done under the circumstances. It might be asked why I didn't simply tell another man to grab the line?

If I had done this, the response of the second man would probably have been the same. I would have lost the respect of every Negro on that levee - all 185 of them. And the Negroes made the rules, I didn't. I had worked on the plantation for only about three years and everything that I had learned, I had learned from the Negroes - and I learned my lessons well!

In successfully working Negroes, it was absolutely necessary to have their respect. There were white men who could not do this and therefore could not keep Negro labor. If a white man conducted himself in a manner that the Negroes did not respect, they considered him a "peckerwood." Of course, there were rich "peckerwoods" as well as poor ones. A man of this type had come from Alabama and bought a plantation adjoining Readland Plantation. He could not get along with the Negro labor and it wasn't very long until he had no labor at all. So he went back to Alabama and brought in quite a number of white families. They didn't stay long. They couldn't live under the existing conditions - poor housing, mud, and the mosquitoes finally ran them out.

We loaded onto the barge as soon as our replacements got off and were taken to Arkansas City where trucks were waiting to take us home. Each man was paid $36, $3 a day for the ten days he worked on the levee, and $3 for each day going and coming. This was a good little sum of money at that time. On the plantation they earned only $1 a day. In all probability, none had as much as $36 very many times in their whole lives. The paymaster had no list of the Negroes who had money coming so I stood there and identified those who were to be paid.

That same night I took George Cracraft's Model T Ford and went to Eudora. I hadn't been in town very long when Walton Matthews, the City Marshal, came up to me and asked if I had my gun. I said that I did and he asked me to go help him arrest Charlie Ambers and I agreed. Charlie, a Negro who ran a taxicab, was known as a "bad nigger."

We went over to May's Drugstore where Ambers was at the time and Walton walked up to him and said, "Charlie, you're under arrest." Charlie stepped back, pulled his coat open with both hands and said, "You can kill me right here, I'm not going!" With that he hit Walton, knocking him down and ran out of the door, down the middle of the street — just flying! I shot at him five times and missed him with every shot. We searched for him, but never did find him.

Later, still the same night, I was driving home in the Model T on the only concrete road that ran through the county. It was the first or second of its kind in the state — just barely wide enough for two cars and it had soft dirt shoulders. I was about halfway home when I saw a man walking toward me on the shoulder on my side of the road. When I got within a few feet of him, he jumped right out in the road in front of me. Though I was not going fast, the car struck him, knocked him down and I ran over him with both wheels. I stopped within a few feet of where he was lying, jumped out of the car, and found him to be unconscious. It happened right in front of a Negro's house and I got him out of bed to come and help me get the injured man into my car and to Dr. Reagon's office at his home in Readland.

Dr. Reagon was a confirmed alcoholic and on this occasion he was pretty drunk. We got the injured man into the office and laid him on the couch. His right arm was broken between the elbow and the wrist. He had a gash on his head and he was still unconscious. Dr. Reagon left to get some splints for the broken arm but never returned. Later we found out that he had passed out and fallen in a ditch.

The Negro who was helping me and I put splints on the broken arm using some shingles left over from repairing a roof, pulled the arm out straight on a chair we had placed beside the couch, wrapped the shingles with cotton putting one on the bottom and one on the top, and tied it up pretty good. We then cleaned his head and, in a little bit, he regained consciousness. We knew where the man lived, so we got him back in the car and took him home. He was in pretty good shape by the time we got there, but we went in the house and saw that he got to bed all right.

The next morning I went up to Dr. Reagon's and told him what had happened and asked him to go see the man to check him over. Doc was sober then and later that day told me that everything looked good; the arm looked like it was completely straight and the wrapping I had put on it looked like it would hold.

In due time the arm healed nicely, just as straight as it could be. You couldn't tell it had been broken. He said he was drunk when the accident happened and he didn't remember anything at all about it. He did not blame me for the accident, but I took care of him until he was able to go to work again.

Setting all of this down here in a manner exactly as it happened may sound as if I was very callous of human life, and at the time I was. I was 23 years of age and tough as a boot both mentally and physically. I had no family life and had received little schooling and teaching from any source except what I taught myself. What I had received in the army over a period of two years was on how to kill someone that I didn't know, especially how to kill him with a bayonet in a muddy trench; someone, who in all probability would have been a good friend under different circumstances. I still have in my possession, a trench knife, the most vicious weapon I ever saw, which I brought home from France. It is good for only one purpose, and that is, to kill a person.

At the end of that long day, having had three encounters which might have been very exciting to most people, I was not physically tired and remained as unemotional as ever. The struggle for my life on top of the levee, assisting in the attempt to make an arrest resulting in gunfire, the accidental running over a person with an automobile — still an unforgettable day!

Chapter IX

On To Law School

Things on the plantation grew from bad to worse that year of 1922. It was very wet, raining a good part of the time. The crops could not be worked properly and there was no logging contract. I was twenty three years of age and becoming dissatisfied as I did not see any future in raising cotton, and I didn't want to spend the rest of my life as a riding boss or plantation manager. At the wages I made, I couldn't ever save enough to acquire a place of my own, so I thought I had better get out and get to doing something else while I was still young. I talked the matter over with George, who was a close family friend, and he agreed with me.

After the crops were laid by, I quit my job, decided to loaf around a while and went to Eudora where I got a room and began thinking about my future. I thought about going to Little Rock to see if I could get in Arkansas Law School , a night school I had heard about. On the other hand, my first love was for horses and cattle and I thought about going out west, getting a job as a cowboy and eventually owning my own ranch.

But I finally decided on law school. I figured that if I failed at that I could still go out west; but if I went out west first and failed, I would probably be a failure forever. I planned to go to Little Rock around Christmas time to try to get accepted into law school the first of the year.

I stayed in Eudora for a while and while I was standing on a corner one day in October, Mr. Charlie Hendricks, a big logging contractor in that area, came up to me. After engaging in conversation for a time, he offered me a job as foreman of his logging camp. This was a pretty good job, paying much more money than I had been making on the plantation. But I declined the job telling him of my decision to go to law school in Little Rock.

A few days after talking to Mr. Hendricks I was thinking the matter over, changed my mind, and decided to take the foreman's job. Mr. Hendricks had taken a job to get out a large tract of timber in an area the other side of Mason Lake beyond Lake Village. A temporary railroad track, called a "dummy line," had been built out into the woods for several miles to facilitate the removal of millions of feet of timber for the Chicago Mill and Lumber Company. I borrowed the Model-T from George and drove as far as I could to a trestle across a bayou. I walked the rest of the distance, about four miles, out to the logging camp but Mr. Hendricks was not there. If he had been, my entire life would have been different as, on the way back to Eudora I again changed my mind and decided to go to law school.

But hunting was on my mind for the immediate future. I had some good friends that I hunted with, Bob and Dyke Carlton, Roy Matthews and Jim Chairs, all of them living near Eudora. We got together, made plans and went deer hunting. We set up camp on Weaver's Bayou about twelve miles from Eudora. None of us had any money. I had about one hundred and fifty dollars that I had saved, but I figured I would need that money to get set up in Little Rock.

Our hunting camp consisted of one tent about fourteen feet by sixteen feet, a cast-iron skillet, a Dutch oven and a coffee pot. We filled oat sacks with straw for bedding and we had a few blankets for cover. We built a fire right in front of the tent to get as much benefit from the heat as possible. We didn't have much to eat, just some sweet potatoes, flour and the other things it took to make biscuits as we figured on killing our meat. None of us considered this rough going to be any hardship.

All of us had horses and we had seventeen hounds — which gave us one of our main problems. It rained a good part of the time and we could not keep the hounds out of the tent, and we all got the mange from them sleeping on our straw bedding.

One needs dogs to hunt deer in that part of the country or one would never see a deer. In hunting deer with hound dogs, we rode horseback with the dogs following us. When we got to a place where we expected to find a deer, we spread out and by siccing the dogs, and whooping and hollering, we caused them to go to hunting. That is, trying to find a trail by the scent made by deer not many hours before.

When a dog hit upon such a scent, he would give forth a bark showing that he had hit a trail and the rest of the dogs would go to him immediately. If a trail was several hours old, not all of the dogs could smell it. But those dogs having the better noses would work it out, barking when they could smell it pretty good. Our best dog for finding a trail and working it out was a black and tan bitch we called, Old Mary.

In all probability, the deer that had passed along there several hours previously (about daylight) would have found a good hiding place in a briar thicket and laid down. And the chances are it was a buck because the scent left by him would be much stronger than a doe. Of course, the buck would know that the dogs were on his trail and in many instances he would stay in his bed until the dogs were very close to him. Perhaps he would be thinking or hoping or sensing or doing whatever deer do, perhaps believing, that the dogs would lose the trail before they got to him. In any event, when the dogs got close enough, he would get up and start running. This was called "jumping the deer." At that point the dogs would have a fresh hot trail, start barking loudly and light out after the deer. We hunted on our horses, staying with the dogs, trying to anticipate where the deer would run and cut him off. Taking a position on a "stand" was too dull for us. But most hunters did take "stands."

On the afternoon of the third day it was raining hard and we still hadn't killed anything. We were all in the tent and suddenly heard noises outside. We went out and there was a wagon pulled by a couple of mules, driven by a local man and four hunters who had come over from El Dorado, Arkansas, to hunt deer. They didn't know much about hunting, had not made proper arrangements and had no dogs. When they had arrived in Eudora and somewhat saw the score, they were told where we were camped. They hired this local man to drive them and their gear out and asked if they could hunt with us. Thinking they might have some food along, we told them it would be just fine.

We pitched in and helped set up their camp, got them fixed real good, and in the process did see a lot of food. That night both camps fixed supper not very far apart but they said nothing about eating with them. The same thing happened the next morning at breakfast.

We put them on stands where they would have a chance to kill something. That morning we killed a deer but they didn't, and we all came into camp at noontime. We dressed our deer and started cooking some of it — we were hungry! That venison hadn't been cooking very long when the other men suggested that it would be a good idea if we all pooled our groceries and ate together, just what we had wanted in the first place. Those hunters stayed with us about four or five days, killed some game, had a good time and left for home.

Our own hunt lasted for about a month. It was in the late fall so it was all over before Christmas and we went back to Eudora. I sold my shotgun and saddle, drew what money I had out of the bank, caught the train for Little Rock and went about getting admitted to the Arkansas Law School.

Judge T.N. Robertson was in charge of admissions at the law school and he asked me about my prior education. I told him that up to this time I had received no formal education beyond the third grade. He said that in order to be admitted to the school, I would have to show the equivalent of a high school education. I went to the Commissioner of Education at the State House there in Little Rock and told him of my dilemma. I asked him to give me a test to show the level of my education, which he did and I passed without any trouble. In fact, he said I had the equivalency of a pretty good college education.

Even though I had quit school in the third grade, I did not neglect my own education. The Little Rock Public Library was not far from Blass' and just about every day at noon hour I went to the library and read, read, read. I read the classics, history, geography, and I was learning math at Blass'. I got an education because I liked to do those things that were educational - not because I realized the need of an education. I just happened to be interested in reading and doing. One thing that served me well was my good memory. When I saw anything, heard anything, or read anything, I remembered it.

I was given the required certificate which I then presented to Judge Robertson and was admitted to the law school in January of 1923; *winning against the odds!*

I then went back to Blass' to look for a job. I talked to Mr. Ike Kempner, one of the top officials, and told him that I intended to go to law school at night. I asked him for a job where I could get off at four o'clock in the afternoon so that I would have a little time to study before classes and he gave me a job in the carpet and drapery department.

There, I learned a good deal about rugs including Chinese and Orientals. Occasionally a rug dealer would come from New York with trunks full of Oriental rugs, and these rugs were put on display and he would do the selling. I would help him handle the rugs and I learned a good deal about the quality of the Orientals. They ranged in price from a few hundred dollars to several thousand. There are machine made "American Orientals" that are good and beautiful and it takes an expert to tell the difference between these and a genuine Oriental. The same thing is true of the Navajo blankets of today.

I got off from work at 4 o'clock and had no trouble in law school. I was able to read for three hours before the starting class at seven o'clock, then after school I would study for about two hours more. Fortunately, with my good memory and being extremely interested, I remembered just about all of what I read, including the "Rules of Evidence" and the "Exceptions to the Rules." This was the subject I liked best and perhaps the reason I became a trial lawyer.

Ordinarily it took two years to finish law school. Classes, with usually about twenty students in each class, were held in the Pulaski County Courthouse; three nights a week for the juniors and three nights for the seniors. But I started in the middle of the year so I had to go back and pick up what I had missed. Hence, I went to school six nights each week. I was pretty well caught up by the end of the school year, studied all that summer and continued to attend classes six nights a week the next year. After actually going to school only one and a half years, I graduated at the head of the class in June, 1924, and made the valedictory address at the graduation exercises.

A short time later the written bar examinations were given in the Senate Chamber at the State Capitol. There were men taking the exam there who had graduated from Harvard and other big law schools. I made the top grade of 98 on my exam. I only missed part of one question and that was on my favorite subject — evidence. I later taught the subject at the Arkansas Law School.

Later, my brother, Harry, and my sister, Lucile, also became lawyers. And I feel that my sister, "Gallie" (Marion), would have made a good lawyer, but she preferred more of a private life.

At this point I would like to digress and say that I was very fortunate to have been able to attend the Arkansas Law School. It was one of the best in the United States, bar none, including Harvard. And, after thirty-five years of active practice in addition to fifteen years on the Arkansas Supreme Court and, having come in contact with lawyers from many law schools, I know whereof I speak.

The faculty at the school consisted of outstanding judges and lawyers who volunteered their time and recieved no pay. In fact, they wouldn't have done it for money. They considered it an honor to be asked to teach. And, of course, we used standard textbooks. There was Judge John Martineau who taught equity. He was Chancellor of the Chancery Court in Little Rock. He later became governor of the state and, still later, a judge of the United States District Court for the Eastern District of Arkansas.

Judge J.H. Carmichael was Dean of the school. He was absolutely dedicated, a top lawyer and a good teacher. And I have already mentioned Judge T.N. Robertson, the Admissions Officer, also a dedicated, very fine lawyer and a good teacher. Judge John W. Wade, Judge of the First Division of the Pulaski Circuit Court, which was the Division that handled criminal cases exclusively, taught criminal law. Archie House, a member of the Rose

Firm, was recognized throughout the State as a top lawyer and taught the subject of Evidence. There was also Harry Trieber, a member of one of the best firms in the state and son of the U.S. District Judge. And there were others, equally as good. All in all, it was a great school!

Immediately upon being admitted to the bar, I quit my job at Blass', rented an office from another lawyer, Mr. Fred Snodgress, right across the street from the Federal Building on Second Street, and hung out my shingle.

Chapter X

Judge Jacob Trieber

During the first year I practiced law, my office was just across the street from the Federal Building, the location of the United States District Court. I hung out a sign which said, "Sam Robinson, Lawyer." It measured about twelve inches by twenty-four inches and was fastened to the building extending out over the sidewalk. I got quite a few clients with that sign — people who were looking for just any lawyer and saw it.

My very first case was defending an old gentleman, Dr. Westbrook, who sold eyeglasses by traveling through the countryside going from house to house. The legislature passed a law requiring peddlers of eyeglasses to have a license, but the law provided that all those currently engaged in the business could obtain a license by merely applying for it by a certain date. This old gentleman had failed to apply and continued to sell eyeglasses. He was arrested, saw my shingle, and retained me to defend him. I simply got him to apply for a license and he was acquitted.

My second case was defending a middle-aged doctor from the northern part of the state who had been charged in Federal Court with selling morphine to an addict. The facts of the case were that a morphine addict, Louis Moore, had gone to the doctor's office seeking the morphine which he told the doctor he needed badly on account of his addiction and physical condition. He also told the doctor he had gonorrhea and tuberculosis and that he was on his way to Hot Springs to seek a cure. He begged the doctor for the shot he needed. The doctor, recognizing the symptoms and realizing Moore needed help, gave it to him.

Moore went back to the doctor's office the next morning saying he had failed to get out of town and was again in bad shape. He prevailed upon the doctor to help him once more. The doctor charged Moore two dollars for each shot. Just after Moore left the second time, a federal narcotics agent entered the office, arrested the doctor and took from him the marked money Moore had paid him.

I knew Moore well as he was one of the Dirty Dozen gang I was acquainted with in my youth. I had seen him occasionally through the years and I knew he was an addict. I was able to bring out in the trial that the federal agent in the case had Moore working with him as an undercover agent, or maybe "stool pigeon" would be a better description. The agent was furnishing Moore with the drugs he needed, but would let him get in very bad condition for the want of a shot before sending him in to a doctor's office so that Moore would look very much the part he was to play.

I was really up against it for a defense in this case, but about a month before the case came to trial, I happened to be reading a borrowed *Harvard Law Review*. I saw a note concerning a case which had recently been decided by the United States Supreme Court which held that a doctor who administers morphine to an addict for the purpose of relieving a condition incident to addiction does not violate the law. The style of the case is *Linder v. the Unites States*. I shall never forget it — it fit my case like a glove. At the trial I was able to prove all the facts necessary to bring the case within the holding in the Linder case.

The judge in the case was Judge Jacob Trieber, whose son had taught me at the Arkansas Law School. In the courtroom at the old Federal Building the judge's bench was up quite high. The court reporter's desk sat right up against the bench and the judge could not see the court reporter from his seat. In those days, the defense attorney had to make arrangements with the court reporter to have the case reported. I am sure that Judge Trieber did not know until a little too late that I was having the case reported.

After Judge Trieber had given his instructions to the jury, I requested that he give the instruction I had prepared, telling him it was based on the Linder case and that it used the exact language of the Supreme Court decision made just a short time before. "Yes, I am familiar with that case," Judge Trieber said, "and

Judge…must have been out of his mind when he wrote that opinion." Judge Trieber was one of the few judges that would have even known of the Linder case. At that point of time, it had not as yet appeared in any of the reports.

I then made my objection to the court's refusal to give the requested instruction and handed the written version to the court reporter, asking that it be made a part of the record. It was only then that Judge Trieber realized that the case was being reported so that it could be appealed to a higher court. Judge Trieber, perhaps remembering what he had said about the Supreme Court Justice who wrote the Linder case, stopped the retiring jury and gave them my instruction. It amounted to an instruction of not guilty and the defendant was promptly acquitted.

Judge Trieber was a Jew from Germany who had come here as a teen-ager. He was never able to rid himself of a strong German accent. All of his w's were v's and he started most of his sentences with "Vell" as in "Vell, Mr. Robinson…."

I think he was a fine judge, although many lawyers, even while recognizing Judge Trieber's ability, did not like him. Before every trial at which he was to preside, Judge Trieber reviewed the pleadings and the law pertaining to the case. He was thoroughly familiar with each case before he walked into the courtroom and God help the lawyer who did not have his case well prepared! Judge Trieber really let an unprepared lawyer have it, right in the presence of the jury and the spectators, leaving many a lawyer embarrassed and with an extreme dislike for him.

Frank French, a young lawyer starting practice at the same time as I, was trying a case before Judge Trieber who, at one point said to French, "Vell, this is no police court," implying French's presentation better belonged in police court. This really shook Frank and made me plumb G--d--- mad. I thought to myself that I would have replied, "No, they have a jury in this court," implying that that was the only difference, that the judges were the same. But I was always prepared and he never did get after me.

In the same period of time, a friend came by the office and asked if I knew that a mutual friend of ours was in jail in Pine

Bluff. He was charged with embezzling funds from the Lake Village Post Office. In a few days I heard the man had been moved from Pine Bluff to Little Rock and that his case was pending in Federal Court.

I went to see him in jail and he told me he had gotten to playing poker and had taken one hundred and fifty dollars of Post Office funds which he then lost during a game. He had started paying the money back, already replacing fifty dollars, when the shortage was discovered by a postal auditor. His arrest followed.

The man said he had told the postal authorities all about it and that they told him if he pleaded guilty they would try to get him a short sentence, but that a plea of not guilty would get him a long stay in the penitentiary. Therefore, he said, he was going to plead guilty. Although I was not defending him, I thought I would see what I could do in his behalf.

At that time, early in my practice of law, I thought that the fact that he had started paying the money back might show that he had no felonious intent in the first place. A necessary element of any felony is - intent. I thought I would go talk with Judge Trieber about the matter and explain my thinking that there was no felonious intent. The very fact that I even went to the Judge, especially Judge Trieber, to talk about a case shows how green I was — a proposition of "fools venturing where angels fear to tread."

But Judge Trieber heard everything I had to say and then said, "Vell, the case hasn't been tried yet. I can't talk to you about it. The District Attorney has a right to be heard." I left thinking I had done everything that could be done and that was the end of the matter as far as I was concerned.

About two weeks later the Clerk of the Court called me at my office across the street and said that I should get right over there at once, that court was being held up for me, although I had no idea why. I went as fast as I could. When I arrived in the courtroom everything was at a standstill and there before the bench of Judge Trieber stood my friend.

"Vell, Mr. Robinson," Judge Trieber said, "vat about this case?" I knew this was my cue to do something. I spoke up and told the court everything I had said in private two weeks earlier. Judge Trieber then said, "Vell, if I give him ninety days and credit for time already spent in jail (which was more than ninety days), vill I not hear any more about this case?" I replied, "Your Honor, you will not hear any more about this case." My friend walked out of the courtroom with me.

Judge Trieber did not always come off in the best light. Colonel Murphy was a wonderful trial lawyer and in a mail robbery case, he reversed Judge Trieber four times. In each of the four distinct trials, the defendant was convicted. Each time, Colonel Murphy appealed the case to the Court of Appeals, and each time Judge Trieber was reversed, thus calling for another trial. Colonel Murphy would manage to make Judge Trieber mad, causing him to make an error. At one point, Colonel Murphy was arguing a point of law to Judge Trieber in open court and was quoting from one of the Judge's own law books. Judge Trieber said, "But that is not the law." Colonel Murphy had the book in his hand, he tore out the page and said to Judge Trieber, "If it is not the law, you ought not to have it in your book."

On another occasion Senator Caraway, a United States Senator from Arkansas, was defending a case in Judge Trieber's court. Senator Caraway was also a wonderful trial lawyer and he had been a prosecuting attorney in the northeastern part of Arkansas before going to the United States Senate. It was said that he had never lost a case as prosecuting attorney.

On the occasion referred to, Senator Caraway was representing a defendant in a criminal case. During the trial, the District Attorney asked a government witness to identify the defendant who was sitting at the counsel table. The witness, for some reason, did not want to identify the defendant and began looking around the courtroom. Judge Trieber spoke up and sarcastically said, "Vell, look down among the lawyers and you may see him." Senator Caraway jumped to his feet and said, "Yes, look up on the bench; you may see him." If it had been any other lawyer, Judge Trieber would have given him a hard way to go, but he was not about to take on Senator Caraway.

One of the jokes I remember from this time concerned a cross-eyed judge who had three defendants before his bench. The judge said to the first man, "Guilty or not guilty?" The second man answered, "Not guilty." The judge said, "I wasn't talking to you." The third man said, "I didn't say anything."

Another of my early cases was defending a young woman charged with selling morphine to a government agent. I suppose she came to me because her father and I knew each other and she emphatically denied having committed the offense.

She was very nice looking and the day before the trial she was at my office and wore a very flattering long sleeved dress. I told her how nice she looked and said to wear that or a similar dress the next day, that appearance was important. The next morning she came to my office a good while before court. She had on a short-sleeved dress and it revealed a portion of a large tattoo on her shoulder. The jury would have surely convicted her just because she had a tattoo. But fortunately, she had enough time to go home and change.

A narcotics agent testified that at 5th and Scott Streets, he paid her four hundred dollars in marked money for morphine. Another agent testified that he had arrested her one block away, intending to recover the marked money, but it was not on her. Both agents testified that they had handled the case in this manner because they thought it would make a better case with one agent paying the defendant and another taking the marked money off her just a few minutes later.

In her testimony, she stoutly denied the charge and stated she had never seen either of the narcotics agents before. There was also the suspicion that the agents might have kept the money themselves. The way the situation developed, the government's case was pretty weak and there was a verdict of not guilty.

Another time I defended two elderly men who were addicts and were charged with illegal possession of morphine. They were guilty, but I worked out a satisfactory plea for them. These two cases and that of the doctor were the only narcotics cases I ever defended and all happened in my first year of practice.

Mr. Ike Kempner, one of the officials at Blass' who had befriended me during my years there, recommended me to the Arkansas Transfer Taxi Company to represent their cab drivers in police court, mostly for speeding. There was a running feud between the drivers of this company and the police and as a result, I was in police court just about every morning representing one or more drivers. I gained a lot of experience fighting these cases.

Meanwhile, I also hung around the court of Judge Wade who taught the course in criminal law when I attended the Arkansas Law School, and I tried to be looking right at him when he was about to appoint counsel for a defendant. He did appoint me to defend a lot of cases and I was able to get a small fee for most of them. In any of the cases in which I was appointed to defend someone, I made it clear that I would do my best regardless of no fee, but that a fee would be accepted if he could pay it, and in almost all the cases I got a small fee.

On one occasion I was talking to a Negro defendant about a fee and he told me that he thought his aunt would help him. She lived in Lake Providence, Louisiana, not far from Readland Plantation. I debated with myself a good while as to whether I should even risk the cost of a long distance phone call to talk to her, but finally decided to do so. She agreed to help her nephew saying she would be in my office in Little Rock in a few days. Sure enough, she was.

She was a mulatto, dressed expensively, and was wearing good jewelry. In talking to her, I learned that she ran a red-light house in Lake Providence and was very able and willing to pay a fee to me for representing her nephew. He was charged with armed robbery and it was going to be a tough case. I did not know what would be a reasonable fee under the circumstances, this being very early in my career. I had never received a fee like the one that I could get for this case and finally, just out of the blue, I told her the fee would be three hundred dollars. Without batting an eye, she opened her purse and peeled off three one-hundred dollar bills from a big roll. I worked hard on that case, as I did in all cases, and the man was acquitted.

I had nothing to do with the following matter other than as a spectator, but I relate it here to further illuminate the times in which I was a young lawyer in Little Rock.

A little white girl about twelve years of age disappeared and a week or so later her body was found in the belfry of a church in downtown Little Rock. She had been raped and murdered. Not long after the officers started working on the case, they arrested a Negro about eighteen years of age, the son of the janitor at the church. There was evidence showing that he was guilty beyond a reasonable doubt.

The city was in an uproar over the crime. The youth was in the jail at City Hall and a large crowd gathered there at Markham and Broadway demanding he be turned over to them. Jim Pitcock, who had been a peace officer for a good part of his life, was Chief of Detectives and he was tough. He and several other officers walked out to the top of the steps on the Broadway side of the building, putting them about six feet above the crowd, and ordered the mob to disperse. Pitcock told them that if they didn't get the hell away, a Goddamn big ass-kicking was going to take place then and there. The mob knew that he meant what he said and left.

A short time later, with a large number of people still mad about the rape and murder of the little girl, a Negro escaped from the county farm west of Little Rock. He was reported to have attacked a white woman who was driving a wagon on what is now Highway 10. The report of the attack spread through the city like wildfire and the Negro was captured by a mob from a hiding place in the top of a tree.

Many people were going to see what had taken place. I ran across Carl Bailey who was Deputy Prosecuting Attorney, and another person at 2nd and Spring. Later Carl became Prosecuting Attorney and still later, Governor of Arkansas. We all went out in Carl's car to what was then Hayes Street and is now University.

At about Eighth Street, a mob of two to three thousand people had hanged the Negro from the cross arm of a telephone pole. We had been there only a minute or so when the husband of the woman supposedly attacked, ran up and discharged a shotgun at the dead man's head. The body was then taken down and thrown across the back end of a Jordan roadster, between the body of the car and the spare tire. The car was driven to about 8th and Main where the body was thrown on the pavement, tied to the car and dragged north on Main Street to Markham; then west on Markham to Broadway past City Hall; and south on Broadway to Ninth Street where the body was cut loose from the automobile, saturated with gasoline and burned. It was the worst thing I ever saw. The next day, the papers quoted Sheriff Mike Haney as saying it had been an "orderly mob."

This episode reminds me of a series of rapes which took place in Little Rock when I was about twelve years old. The rapes were committed at night by a man who forced his way into houses of white women and he shot several of his victims. He was referred to as "Jack the Shooter" and I rode a streetcar with one of the victims who still had a scar on her neck where she had been shot.

The rapes went on for some time and it got to the point that the entire city was alarmed. Many were carrying guns and patrolling the streets at night. Finally, one night there was a hot pursuit of a suspect. The man ran onto the back porch of a house and tried to get in through a window. The house belonged to a very large Negro named Sam Collins who had just come from work and was laying across his bed in the room the fleeing man was trying to enter. Collins could hear the noise, but it was very dark and he could not see anything. He just aimed his gun in the direction of the window and fired, hitting the intruder in the chest. The wounded man ran to the back fence but could not make it over. He fell dead.

The body was taken to the Healy and Roth Mortuary and many people went to view it including me. The man's face was that of a Negro, but it was covered with some kind of white salve to make it appear as if he were a white man.

Chapter XI

Unusual Cases

About a year after I entered the practice of law, Mr. Bob Rogers, a leading criminal lawyer in Arkansas who was then elderly and past his prime, offered me a partnership with him. I thought the matter over and decided to accept his proposition. He was to get two-thirds of the fees and I was to get one-third.

The first murder case we had after the formation of the partnership was the defense of a Dr. Stanley who was charged with shooting and killing a young man at a dance. The trouble took place at Ironton, a settlement in Pulaski County north of Little Rock, where both the doctor and the young man lived. In addition to being the community doctor, Dr. Stanley was also the Constable. Nevertheless, he was convicted of manslaughter.

We had quite a few cases in the one year of the partnership. I was making a living with thirty percent of the fees, but as many of the cases were coming to me as to Mr. Rogers. I did not want to continue with the same financial arrangement and Mr. Rogers did not want to change it, so we dissolved the partnership.

I had been out of law school and practicing for about three years when I was retained by Paul Talley, an established Little Rock lawyer, to defend his brother, Jim. He was charged with rape at Hot Springs in Garland County. Jim Talley had a job with the United States government overseeing the dipping of cattle in a program designed to eradicate the Texas fever tick.

The tick had caused a great deal of damage among cattle throughout the southern states and the government had constructed concrete dipping vats in convenient places in each county. Cattle owners were required to dip their stock every two weeks to kill the ticks. After a tick is hatched, it will die within two weeks unless it can attach itself to an animal to feed off the blood.

On the occasion in question, Talley was dipping some cattle about twenty-five miles from his home. While there, a young woman about eighteen years old came up and asked him if she could ride home with him in his Model T as she lived just across the Ouachita River from Talley. He agreed to let her ride and, after work was over, they got in the Model T and started home.

Talley said the girl was big and buxom and that they had not gone very far before she was rubbing up against him, especially her breasts. The result was that he and the girl had sex — six times —before they got to the river near Talley's home where he was going to put the girl over the river on his horse. He stopped at his house to get the horse and found his wife and children were not there, so he wrapped a quart of moonshine in a yellow slicker which he then tied to the back of the saddle. It had been raining and when he and the girl got to the river, it could not be crossed on horseback. So they drank some moonshine and had sex one more time. The girl was pretty drunk by then and, when Talley could not do anything with her, he just left her there and went home.

When the girl got dressed, due to her being so drunk, she put her dress on hind part before and inside out. But she did manage to get to a nearby house and came around to herself with people questioning her as to what had happened. Then she said she had been raped by Talley. The people took her to the prosecuting attorney with the result that Talley was indicted.

On the way from the dipping vats to the river, Talley and the girl had stopped and talked to several people. At one point they had gone in one person's house and had even visited a little. We had all these people as witnesses to prove that the girl had made no complaint about being mistreated. And Talley testified that they had had sex several times before meeting some of these people.

But the girl testified that she had only been raped once, down at the river. Evidently someone had told her that it wouldn't do to say she had been raped seven times, especially over a distance of twenty-five miles. Especially when they had stopped to talk to several people and she had said nothing. Admitting to this would have made the State's case very weak. But it was a horse of a different color if they engaged in sex only once, so she continued to deny that they had had sex seven times and it was just her word against his.

During a recess, a deputy prosecuting attorney who was not in this case came to me, and told me that the girl had told him that she had been raped seven times. I asked him if he would testify to it. He agreed and I put the girl back on the stand for further cross-examination. I asked her if she had told the deputy prosecuting attorney that she had been raped seven times and she denied it. I then put the deputy on the stand for his opposing testimony. The jury was not out long before bringing in a verdict of not guilty.

During the preparation of this case, I heard that the girl had talked to her grandmother about the matter. The grandmother lived at a settlement called "Possum Kingdom" west of Hot Springs. I went to see the old lady but could not get all the way to her house in my T-Model Ford and had to walk about a mile.

When I arrived at the house, there were several old ladies sitting on the porch shelling peas. I asked for the grandmother of the girl and one of the women spoke up and identified herself. I then told her that I was a lawyer representing the man charged with raping her granddaughter and I would like to speak to her privately. She said there was no need in talking privately and asked what I wanted to know. I told her that I understood that her granddaughter had talked with her about the alleged crime and I would like to know what she had to say. The old lady replied, "Well, the only thing she had to say to me was, 'Grandma, are all men's peters kind of blue?'" The other old ladies just kept on shelling peas, I asked no further questions and walked back to my car. And of course, I did not have her subpoenaed as a witness.

My practice continued to grow and about 1928 I formed a partnership with Ed Dillon, who had just been elected to the Arkansas State Senate. We had several enjoyable years as law partners. Ed had a great sense of humor and was good at making clever, witty remarks.

On one occasion, we had been out at the State Capitol and as we were getting into our car, a young woman rushed up and asked if she could ride to town with us saying she was on her lunch hour and needed to pick up her watch which had been repaired. Ed replied, "Certainly, but what you really need is a good Gruen." She laughed and rode into town with us.

Another time Ed and I were walking down the street and we met a friend who was also a friend of Carl Bailey. Bailey was running for governor and there were many uncomplimentary rumors circulating about him. Our friend said to Ed, "Ed, you certainly don't believe all those rumors being circulated about Carl, do you?" Ed replied, "Why, I certainly do! I started most of them myself."

Ed really didn't like Bailey. When Bailey was Attorney General of Arkansas, Ed represented Lucky Luciano, the New York mobster, at a hearing in the Federal Court in Little Rock. The state of New York was trying to extradite Luciano who was staying at Hot Springs. Bailey was, of course, representing the State of Arkansas and he said in open court that he had been offered fifty thousand dollars to stay out of the case. The statement really made Ed mad and he said, "It must have been confederate money, wasn't it, Carl?"

In the course of one case, Ed was down at the jail which had been built in 1880 and, although only fifty years old at the time, was called the Old Jail. There were no facilities such as a private room where a lawyer could talk to his client. If a lawyer was going to have an extended visit with a client and did not want to stand up at the bars of the cell door, the jailer would let him inside the cell with the prisoner. When the lawyer was ready to leave, he would rattle on the door of the cell, which was on the second floor, and could normally be heard downstairs at the turnkey's office. Someone would then come up and let the lawyer out of the cell.

But this time Ed stayed quite long. The turnkey forgot he was there, closed the door between the floors and when Ed rattled the door, could not hear him. After several minutes with no response, Ed shouted, "I want out of here!" A Negro woman in another cell responded with "Dey all duz."

One time when Ed was running for re-election, he was campaigning in the little town of Levy, a suburb of North Little Rock, by going into downtown businesses asking for votes. He asked one storekeeper for his vote and the man, who was probably mad at Ed because of some bill he had voted on, told him "Hell no, I won't vote for you! I wouldn't vote for you if you were the only man in the race!" Ed's response was to very calmly take out his notebook and pencil and, while writing, say to the man, "I'll put you down as lukewarm."

Ed continued on to other businesses down the street, then crossed over and worked his way back up the other side. When he was across the street from the angry shopkeeper, the man came out of his store and hollered to Ed, "I'm going to vote for you."

I don't think there was ever a better man, a more moral man, that ever lived than Ed Dillon. He finally became disabled with Parkinson's disease. We dissolved the partnership and I went on alone. Ed's son, Ed Dillon, Jr., is now one of the leading lawyers in Little Rock.

When I began the practice of law, I would just take any kind of case that came along. But I was kept busy in the practice of criminal law and some of the cases are worth mentioning.

Virgil Williams was charged with murder. He and a man named Wagner had broken out of the Oklahoma penitentiary, stolen an automobile, picked up Wagner's wife and all three of them came to Little Rock. They needed money so they let Wagner's wife out at the small town of Levy, adjacent to North Little Rock. They drove in to Little Rock looking for a place to rob and finally decided on King's Drugstore at 15th and Gaines. But in the middle of the robbery a couple of city detectives just happened to walk in. They saw what was happening, got the drop on Williams and Wagner, put them under arrest and took them to jail. The detectives, of course, didn't know anything about Wagner's wife out at Levy and the two men certainly didn't offer any information.

When the paper came out the next day, Wagner's wife found out about the arrests and within a few days visited her husband and Williams at Pulaski County jail. She managed to slip hacksaws to them and the two men sawed their way out of their cells into what was called the "runaround." They waited there till early the next morning when the jailer came in, knocked him unconscious and went downstairs. There were no other officers at the jail. But Bert Simmons, a deputy sheriff, had left his pistol on a desk. Williams and Wagner took the pistol, went out the front door and finally wound up at the city park in the eastern part of Little Rock where they hid out all day long.

That night there was a band concert at the park and many people were in attendance, some listening to the music from their cars in the parking area. The two-time escapees walked up to a car occupied by a young man named George Chance and his date. The men pointed the pistol at Chance, got in the car and compelled him to drive out of town, ending up at the Confederate Cemetery on the southeast edge of the city. They made Chance drive into the cemetary, get out of the car and were in the process of robbing him of fourteen dollars when again, two city detectives drove up.

One of the detectives was Neil McDermott, a big man who had been a football player and was well-known and very popular. Williams, using Bert Simmon's pistol, became involved in a shoot-out and shot McDermott through the axillary fold of his right armpit. Williams then ran through the cemetery and out onto the highway, right into the arms of another officer. Williams and Wagner were both returned to jail and McDermott died nine days later.

Anyone killing an officer is in deep trouble, but Williams was especially so here because of McDermott's popularity. Both men were charged with murder in the first degree which carried the death penalty or a life sentence. Public sentiment ran high against the two men and their cases were set for trial at an early date.

A few days after McDermott's death, Virgil William's mother came to my office from Oklahoma and wanted to retain me to represent her son. It was going to be a hard case because of the charge against Williams and the popularity of McDermott. In Arkansas, it is murder in the first degree if one kills another person while committing a felony. The usual elements of premeditation, deliberation and malice of forethought do not have to be proven. And after talking with Williams, I knew that a plea of insanity could not be sustained. The only chance I saw was to get him a life sentence rather than death in the electric chair.

I talked with Mrs. Williams for a long time and finally agreed to accept the case for a fee of fifteen hundred dollars. It was the heart of the depression, the mid-thirties, and fifteen hundred dollars was a lot of money. But it was something she said she could pay and told me she would have to go back home to Oklahoma to raise the money. I heard from her some time later; she said she was getting the money together, everything was all right and she would be back in Little Rock before the trial.

In the meantime, I was working on the defense in the case. I managed to see McDermott's hospital record and it appeared he was getting along very well until the ninth day when a lump was discovered in his right armpit. The doctors diagnosed it as an abscess and operated to drain it; but it was not an abscess, rather a large blood clot. The bullet had severed the axillary vein and the clot had formed. The doctors removed the clot, but neglected to tie off the open vein. A piece of the clot got into the vein, went to the heart and killed him. According to medical authority, when a large vein is severed, it should be ligated, or tied off, to keep this very thing from happening.

My defense was that the doctors were negligent for not ligating McDermott's axillary vein, thus causing his death. And for that reason, I argued the jury should give Williams life in the penitentiary rather than the death penalty. I tried to plead him guilty and take a life sentence, but the prosecuting attorney would not agree to this. He was demanding the electric chair, as were all the peace officers and most of the public.

Three days before the trial was to begin, Mrs. Williams arrived and told me she had been unable to raise the money for my fee. After questioning her closely, I came to the conclusion that there never had been any possibility of raising the money, that she had just roped me into taking the case. I told her that under the circumstances, I would not represent her son, especially since the case was such a hard one, with the death penalty a possibility, in fact - a probability. Williams had escaped from the Oklahoma penitentiary, had stolen a car, and was in the act of robbing a drugstore when he was apprehended. He then sawed his way out of his jail cell, knocked the jailer unconscious, stole the deputy's pistol, and was committing another robbery when he shot and mortally wounded a popular police officer. I didn't know of much more that could be against him. About the only thing he didn't do was to rape the date of George Chance.

I told Mrs. Williams that I would inform the court of the circumstances and ask that another lawyer be appointed to defend her son. I immediately went to the courthouse, found Judge Abner McGehee, who was to preside at the trial, and told him of my decision that I would not represent the man free of charge and that he would have to appoint someone else for the defense. Later that afternoon, Judge McGehee called me and said it was too late for anyone else to get ready for the trial, that he was not going to continue the case, and that he would have to appoint me to defend Williams.

I defended the case the best I could, just as if I had been paid a fee. I presented the theory that McDermott died due to negligence of the doctors, but the jury brought in the verdict carrying the death penalty. I knew this might happen and I had been very careful during the course of the trial in preserving the record of anything that could possibly be held in error. At one point I knew the trial court had made an error in admitting into evidence, proof that Williams had committed a crime in Oklahoma by stealing an automobile. I made no big fuss over the matter, just quietly made my objection and saved my exception.

I appealed the case to the State Supreme Court and while the case was pending, I visited Williams in the death house at the penitentiary. The electric chair was in this same building and when a certain door was open, the chair could be seen from the cells. It was a beautiful spring day and the flowers were in bloom all over the penitentiary grounds. Captain Todhunter, who was in charge at that time, let Williams out of his cell and permitted him to come into the yard to talk to me. Williams looked at me, then around the grounds at everything so pretty and said, "I sure hate to go and sit in that chair, but I can do it."

On appeal, the Supreme Court held that the trial court had committed an error in permitting the state to introduce evidence of crimes other than the one for which Williams was being tried. But since the undisputed evidence showed that the defendant was guilty of murder in the first degree, the high court cured the trial court's error by reducing the punishment to a life sentence.

Some time later, McDermott's widow came to me. She said that during William's trial, she was convinced that the doctors were at fault in her husband's death and asked me if she had a case against them. Pulaski County was noted as a poor place for a plaintiff to try a personal injury suit, but I told her I was thoroughly convinced the doctors were negligent and that I would take the case. I filed a suit against both doctors, alleging they were negligent in failing to ligate the axillary vein at the time they removed the blood clot from McDermott's armpit. I had read what the medical textbooks and journals had to say on the subject and I knew I was right. But I had a hard time finding a doctor who would testify to this effect.

One of the doctors was represented by Henry Donham, a great trial lawyer who had been prosecuting attorney. On the morning of the trial, I told Henry that I would dismiss the case against his client if he would get out of the case. He took me up on the proposition. I tried the case against just the one doctor, but that was all right — he had plenty of insurance.

Due to what is known as the "conspiracy of silence", most doctors won't testify against another doctor, even one who is not respected in the medical profession or wouldn't be spoken to on the street. But I finally did find one who would testify that the axillary vein should have been ligated. However, the defense produced eight of the leading doctors in Little Rock who all testified that the operation was done just as it should have been.

The jury, in spite of the testimony of the well known doctors, returned a verdict for Mrs. McDermott in the sum of twenty thousand dollars, the first malpractice judgment ever rendered against a doctor in Pulaski County. It was the largest judgment in any kind of personal injury case in the county up to that time, although Pulaski County was noted as a poor place for a plaintiff to try a personal injury suit.

The losing doctor appealed to the Arkansas Supreme Court where the judgment was reversed and dismissed with the holding that there was not sufficient evidence to sustain the verdict. I was trying another personal injury case at Lake Village when I got the news. I did not get paid for defending Williams and lost the usual fifty percent in Mrs. McDermott's personal injury case — eleven thousand five hundred dollars to be exact and a small fortune at that time. I lost all the way around on these two cases.

While I was in private practice, I tried quite a few personal injury cases. One involved a man named White who worked for the East Arkansas Lumber Company and who operated a press that glued plywood together. He had to pull with all his strength for the press to work properly. In doing this one day, his feet slipped out from under him and a bone near the end of his spine, the sacrum, struck a bolt protruding from the floor.

The injury caused him a lot of pain, but he continued to work for several days. When the pain did not subside, the company sent White to a doctor who made x-rays, but did nothing else. The pain continued and after going to the same doctor a few times over the next several months with no change in his condition, he was sent to the clinic of Dr. Willis Campbell, an orthopedic surgeon in Memphis. Dr. Campbell operated on White and found a "condrosarcoma," a cancer, just inside the sacrum. The cancer was tied into the sacro-plexus and was inoperable. White was sent home to die.

When he got home, he came to see me. The place in the mill where he had worked was wet and slippery and a bolt protruding from the floor constituted a hazard. I thought the company was negligent in allowing this condition to exist. I took the case and filed a suit alleging the negligence as well as alleging that the cancer was caused by the injury.

It would have been far too expensive to get Dr. Campbell to come and testify, but I did have his report. It was not, in itself, admissible as evidence so I took the matter up with Dr. W.S. Smith, a leading surgeon in Little Rock. I explained the situation and he agreed to operate on White, get a specimen of the growth, examine it with the idea of determining the correctness of Dr. Campbell's report, and then testify to the results. Dr. Smith testified that he had found a cancer was present and that it was his opinion that the injury caused the cancer.

During cross-examination, he was asked on what he based his opinion that an injury can cause cancer. Dr. Smith testified that he had just written an article for the *American Medical Association Journal* on this very subject. He had found that a great many Chinese men had cancer of the mouth, lips and throat and that very few, if any, Chinese women had these types of cancer. This was caused by the fact, he testified, that the men ate first while the rice was still steaming hot, injuring the mouth and throat tissues which resulted in cancer. The women, he said, ate later after the rice had cooled.

The defense produced several doctors who testified that an injury would not cause cancer, but the jury found in our favor and returned a judgment for a substantial amount. White lived only a few more months and his family had the benefit of the money awarded in the case.

Another case of considerable interest was that of Bill McGuire who was charged with murder.

A young woman named Elsie worked as a manicurist at the barbershop in Little Rock where I got my hair cut. One morning she was waiting for me when I arrived at my office, early as usual. Elsie told me that her brother, Bill McGuire, had been convicted of murder and was sentenced to death. She asked if I would help him. She had no money to pay a fee, but I said I would see what I could do.

I went directly to the courthouse and found that the time for appeal to the State Supreme Court had not expired. I obtained a copy of the judgment and took it to the court at once, which was sufficient to lodge the case in the Supreme Court and automatically stay the execution.

I ordered a transcript of the trial and, upon a thorough examination, I could not find an error on which I could get a reversal. In fact, there was not much trial and that is what I argued in the Supreme Court. A young, inexperienced lawyer had been appointed to defend Bill and much was left undone. In talking to Bill, I found out that he had served in the First World War when he was sixteen years of age and had an excellent war record. Nothing of this was in the record of the trial.

The evidence in the case was that Bill and another man, Elder Smith, were walking down the street and Bill was carrying a 30-30 Winchester rifle. Without any cause whatsoever, he just up and shot a man through the window of a filling station, killing him. Elder Smith had told officers that it was Bill who did the killing after which he threw the rifle in a creek. The officers found the rifle, arrested Bill and his trial and death sentence followed.

I never did believe that Bill was the one who did the shooting, but he said he was so drunk that he couldn't remember anything about the incident. I decided I was going to have to argue things in the Supreme Court that did not appear in the record, on the grounds that the record did not contain the many things it should have.

One thing I wanted to see was Bill's army record. I tried to get it but was at first, unsuccessful. Joe Robinson, a very influential United States Senator from Arkansas and the vice-presidential candidate on Al Smith's ticket, had an office in Little Rock. He was a good friend of mine and I went to see him. I told him about being unable to get Bill's army record and asked for his help. I went back to my office and within hours the record was on my desk. It must have been flown in as it had to have come from Washington, D.C.

His record showed just what Bill had told me. He had been engaged in a lot of fighting during the war and one of the things I argued in the Supreme Court was that if Bill had committed the crime as shown by the record, he had been taught to kill as a teen-ager in the war. To the best of my knowledge, this is the first time that particular argument was used by the defense in a murder trial. But my arguments did not prevail and the judgment was affirmed.

Governor Marion Futrell had been Chancellor of a Chancery Court in eastern Arkansas and I knew him pretty well. I started working on him to get Bill's death sentence commuted to a life sentence. I went to see him several times, but could not get an answer from him. Just two days before Bill was to be executed, I still had not gotten an answer so I arose real early the next day and was at the governor's house by five a.m. so I would be there when he got up. He invited me in for a cup of coffee, but he still would not give me an answer about commuting Bill's sentence. I was urging him with everything I could, as Bill's execution was now less than twenty-four hours away.

I accompanied him to his office at the Capitol Building and he said he would let me know something in a little while. I sat in the waiting room and saw lunch time come and go. The Governor left, returning late in the afternoon. He then told me that he had decided to commute Bill's sentence. I got his proclamation to that effect and lit out for the state penitentiary at Tucker, Arkansas, arriving there early that evening.

I delivered the proclamation to Jewell Acklin, the warden and we went immediately to the death house to tell Bill. When we walked up to his cell, he was gripping the bars with all his might and when Jewell told him about the commutation, he fainted. Then we could not get into the cell to help him because the man with the keys had gone in to town. But Jewell threw some water through the bars and Bill came around all right. Some years later, during my term as Prosecuting Attorney, Bill was paroled from prison.

Later that night, Jewell invited me to supper at his home at the pen. There were two other men to whom I was introduced by name only, with no clue as to their business there but they looked pretty tough to me. Both had on dark suits and I sized them up as Chicago gangsters who had come down to the pen to see some friends. After supper I found out they were the executioners. I also found out that their father had been the executioner for

Arkansas and several adjoining states before them. They were there for Bill's execution scheduled for the next morning. They were paid by the "head" and appeared to be mad about losing the business.

Chapter XII

"Big-To-Do"

Sometime in the forties while I was Prosecuting Attorney, Katie Cracraft was to be married. She and her brother, Goerge, Jr., had been born while I worked for their father at Readland. The wedding took place at Helena where she and her family then lived. They were well-known and highly respected over a large part of the delta country.

Katie had a huge wedding. All the guests attending could not get in the church, but I was there, down front within the ribbons, because I was so close to the family. The ceremony progressed as usual until the point where the preacher says, "Do you take this woman..." when the groom fainted dead away and fell to the floor. The ushers picked him up and carried him to the side of the church. Katie didn't bat an eye, just walked over and sat by her mother in the first pew. After a few minutes the groom came around, was helped to his feet, and walked back to the altar. Katie joined him and the preacher began again, right from the beginning. When he reached the same place, "Do you take this woman..." the groom fainted again. This time the ushers took him outside where he remained quite a while before he was able to continue.

Meanwhile, two straight chairs were placed in front of the altar and Katie, staying very cool and calm, again sat with her mother. Finally the groom returned, he and Katie sat in the chairs, and the ceremony proceeded without further incident.

Later I learned that this popular couple had attended some forty parties given for them prior to the wedding and, of course, in the delta country there was a lot of drinking. All the members of the wedding party promised Katie they would not take a drink until after the wedding and, in my opinion, what the groom really needed was a good, stiff drink.

I had two children and one Sunday morning I took my daughter, Lucile, who was about four or five years old, down to my office with me. I parked the car at the curb; it was a convertible and I had the top down. When we were leaving to return home, Lucile was sitting in the seat beside me and before I moved the car, a badly crippled man came by right close to Lucile who said, "Oh, Daddy, look at that man!" I am sure the man heard her.

I started up the car and gave Lucile a lecture about referring to anyone's physical disabilities, especially when it could be heard by that person and told her to pretend she didn't notice. We turned the corner at the next street and there on the side walk was another crippled person. As we passed on by him, Lucile turned to me and said, "Daddy, I didn't even see him."

Not long after that I was playing ball with my son, Sam, Jr., and I fell, breaking my arm right at the elbow. Dr. Donald Hays was a real good friend of mine and lived about a mile from my house. He and I both owned horses and often rode together. So he fixed my arm, putting what I thought was an ungodly splint on it. Not only was there a cast that covered my entire arm, but there was also a second cast, a body cast around my chest. The arm was raised to where the elbow was about even with my shoulder and had a brace that went from the arm cast to the body cast to hold the arm in that elevated position. It was summertime, very hot, and all that cast was plumb uncomfortable.

After it had been on my arm a while, I took a notion to cut the cast off my body, do away with the brace, and lower my arm. I sat in a chair and told Aaron Jones, a Negro penitentiary parolee, whom I had defended for murder and who was working for me, to take some pruning shears which were good and sharp and cut the cast off my body. The shears cut the cast real good and it and the brace were soon off. I let the arm down and it felt real good.

I then thought that a kind of window in the upper part of the cast on my arm would let in some air and it would feel still better. Aaron made the cut as directed and it did feel better. Then I thought, why not do the same thing with the lower part of the cast. Aaron dutifully cut that part out and the breeze getting in there really felt even better.

There wasn't anything left holding the cast on my arm except a piece right in the crook of the elbow so I decided to do away with that also, lift my arm out, and see how it felt. Aaron cut, I lifted my arm out of the cast and it immediately began to swell. Right about that time I heard Dr. Hays riding up on his horse. He rode right up to where I was sitting, pieces of cast piled around me, with my swollen arm resting on my knee.

He looked around astounded as I looked up at him with guilt all over my face and asked, "Will this hurt anything?" He glared at Aaron standing there with the shears in his hands and replied, "I don't know, I'm not treating you. Dr. Jones there is treating you. Ask him!" But shortly after, we went down to his office where he applied another cast. This one let my arm hang at my side and there was no body cast, so everything was fine.

I had come across Aaron Jones when he was a hostler on a plantation down the Arkansas River from Little Rock. He had shot and killed his wife with a pistol. According to Jones, he caught her putting strychnine in the mashed potatoes, a heated argument developed, and he shot her. The potatoes were tested and they did contain strychnine. But it was the opinion of the Prosecuting Attorney that Jones had doctored the potatoes himself.

But no one, neither the Prosecuting Attorney nor I could ever find out where the strychnine came from. We went to trial; Aaron was convicted of manslaughter and given a light sentence. In a few months I got him out of the penitentiary on parole and he went to work for me at my home.

I defended another Negro named Jones, Willie Jones, who lived on West Ninth Street in one of the Negro sections of Little Rock. One day there was a crap game at Willie's house and one of the crapshooters was a Negro called "Big-To-Do." He was a real character who had been in trouble several times and was pretty much of a bad actor. But he was the favorite of a well-known, well-liked lawyer in Little Rock named Don Hawthorne.

"Big-To-Do" worked for Don part of the time and Don thought a lot of him.

In the crap game at Willie's, "Big-To-Do" went broke. He did a good deal of mouthing about having lost his money and made some threats, but then he left. After walking about half a block he turned around, came back and knocked on the front door which, of course, was locked with the game in progress.

A shade covered the glass panel on the door and when Willie went to answer the knock, he stooped down and looked under the shade to see who was there. When he did this, "Big-To-Do" shot him through the glass with a .45 automatic. The bullet hit Willie on the bridge of the nose and, due to the position of his head, traveled down through the top of his mouth, through his tongue, into the bottom of his mouth, and lodged in his throat. But it did not knock him out. He staggered over to his bed, got his pistol from under his pillow, and went out the back door. He met "Big-To-Do" rounding the corner on one side of the house. Willie shot and killed him.

It was a clear case of self-defense and I always felt it was due to Hawthorne's influence that the case was even brought to trial. Hawthorne even testified for the prosecution, but there was a verdict of not guilty and Willie recovered from his wounds.

One of my most interesting cases was not as a defense lawyer or Prosecuting Attorney, or even as a Supreme Court Justice. It had to do with an illness of Mrs. Healey (my "then" mother-in- law). She had been in St. Vincent's Infirmary for three months and she had two doctors on her case, one of whom had been at Mayo Clinic in Rochester, Minnesota. The doctors said she was dying and that she would not live for more than ten days, but they never did say what was wrong with her. She was practically in a coma and I think she had just given up.

I had a small ranching operation at the time and I took a notion that a liniment I used on the horses would help my mother-in-law, but I knew the doctors would never consent to this. The family was talking about sending her to Mayo Clinic but I said I wanted to try my liniment and if she wasn't better in three days, they could take her.

I got a small bottle of the liniment and arrived at the hospital real early so I could do the treatment before the doctors got there. I started rubbing her joints with the liniment; her shoulder, her elbows, her knees, her ankles. The liniment had a pretty strong smell but it was not offensive. When I was about halfway through, the two doctors came in and they looked at me with astonishment.

I said, "Well, come on in. I'm just giving her a treatment." One of them smiled, the other one frowned, but I continued with my rubbing. They stayed a few minutes and left without any comment.

When I returned that afternoon I thought she already looked a little better. I gave her another treatment and returned the next morning. She was definitely better and I repeated the procedure that afternoon and the next morning. By that time she looked so good that I told her she would have to get out of bed. She liked to dance, especially the waltz, so I found a small record player and a recording of a good waltz and went back to the hospital. I got her out of bed, started the record player, had her hold me around my neck with both hands, and I waltzed her up and down the smooth floor of the hospital hall. We didn't waltz all that long, but she was a different person.

To make a long story short, when Monday came, instead of going to the Mayo Clinic, she went home and lived twenty-five more years without any trouble.

The following two stories illustrate that the selection of jurors is of the utmost importance. A lawyer cannot be too careful in this respect; different people will reach different conclusions from the same set of facts.

I was representing the principal of a school located out in the country. He was charged with having sexual relations with a girl from his school who was under sixteen years of age and the people of the community were up in arms about the case. Pat Mehaffy, the Prosecuting Attorney, was personally trying the case and he was a good friend of mine.

He felt very strongly that there should be a conviction in the case and we were both being very careful in the selection of the jury. We had exhausted the regular jury panel and when the judge sent the sheriff out to bring in more prospective jurors, Pat and I went for coffee. When we got back to the courtroom, we both noticed a man who had been sent in as a prospective juror. Pat nudged me and said, “Who’s that?” “I don’t know,” I answered.

Pat, as the Prosecuting Attorney, examined him first, didn’t ask too many questions, and passed him to me. I also examined him without asking too many questions. Pat accepted him and I then accepted the man as a member of the jury. After the trial was over, the jury having returned a verdict of not guilty, Pat and I again went to have coffee.

Right in front of the restaurant stood the above-mentioned juror. There was nothing to do but to ask him to have coffee with us. During the ensuing conversation, Pat found out the man was a real good friend of mine and I found out he was Pat’s next door neighbor.

In many cases prospective jurors are privately investigated as to their beliefs, connections, etc., before they ever report for jury duty. Under the system of selecting jurors at that time of which I write, it was not uncommon for people who wanted to serve on juries to manage to be called time and again, especially in the courts that tried criminal cases. And some jurors would get reputations for leaning toward convicting or acquitting a defendant before any evidence was presented.

There was one man who was on juries frequently and had the reputation of wanting to convict on every case, and he was known among lawyers who practiced criminal law. I was trying a case in which this man was called as a juror and I wanted to get the court to excuse him without exhausting one of my challenges. I thought to make the man mad and he might then say something to give cause to being excused by the court.

My first question on voir dire examination was, “Isn’t it a fact that you are on the jury frequently; that you have never voted ‘not guilty’; that the words ‘not guilty’ are not in your vocabulary?” The Prosecuting Attorney vigorously objected to the question. I replied to the objection in a heated manner and we got into a hot argument over the point.

Finally, the court called us to order and sustained the objection. I quickly said, "All right, I'll take him." I had put this juror on the spot and when the jury retired to consider the veredict, he voted, "not guilty."

I have always tried to be discreet and not hurt anybody's feelings. I know, for instance, that one should not speak of ropes in the presence of a person whose father has been hanged. But sometimes you stick your foot in your mouth anyway.

I went to the courthouse one day to file some papers and there was a lady working there whom I had never seen before. She was unattractive, rude and diagreeable. I tended to my business and left.

About halfway back to my office, I met the judge who was responsible for filling that job in the clerk's office. He was a friend of mine and I felt close enough to him to mention that I thought he had made a big mistake giving the job to that woman. I said to him, "Where did you get that woman in the clerk's office? She's certainly not doing you any good." He turned red, grinned, and said, "That's my wife." The only thing I could think to say was, "she acts just like my wife!" I don't think he held my faux pas against me.

Chapter XIII

The Strap

One night as I was about to sit down to supper my phone rang. It was a friend of mine, Troy Meadows, who was calling from police headquarters. He said he had been arrested for being drunk and asked me to come down to the police station and get him out. I left the house immediately although I thought it was strange for him to be calling me on a drunk charge as it was not usually much of a job getting out on bail, just put up twenty-five dollars and that was about it.

Well, when I got there I found out that Troy's being drunk was not the problem and he didn't appear to be all that drunk. He had been in a car with a Mrs. McEachson, a wealthy widow, and she was charged with driving while drunk, an entirely different thing — and she was real drunk.

They were in the office at headquarters and the police had not locked either of them up. Mrs. McEachson was standing up, but leaning on her elbows on the counter holding her head. I was in the process of making their bond when an officer brought in a little short fellow who was also charged with being drunk.

At that time a test for drunkenness was given by using what was called a "drunkometer", a balloon-shaped rubber thing that the one being tested blew into. The officer told the little fellow to blow into the balloon. He picked it up and said, "Why, I'll bust the son-of-a-bitch!" and proceeded to blow as hard as he could. When he did this, he let out a very loud fart. He looked around real sharply at Mrs. McEachson and said, "Why goddamn! If she's that drunk, you ought to throw her ass in jail!" There were several officers there and they all got a big laugh.

But Meadows and Mrs. McEachson never did get off that drunk. About two weeks after they were arrested, he accidentally shot her with a .22 rifle. He told me later that he was demonstrating to her what he would do to Hitler if he had a chance. He didn't know the gun was loaded and shot her in the side. They didn't call a doctor, just wrapped a blanket around her body, and they continued to drink. She died three days later.

I could not represent Troy because I had been elected Prosecuting Attorney and, in all probability, would take office before the case was tried. He pleaded guilty to manslaughter and got a short sentence in the penitentiary. If I had represented him, I would not have allowed him to plead guilty. In my opinion, the shooting was strictly accidental and I am sure I could have proved this fact.

On a dark night, in a block on West Fifth Street in Little Rock where the old Peabody School used to be, a car struck and killed two pedestrians; a Mr. Sanders, who was a well-known businessman, and a Mrs. Mathews, who had formerly been one of my stenographers. It was a hit-and-run and many people were pretty well upset. There was great feeling against the driver of the car, whoever it might be.

A few days later a policeman was walking down West Second Street and saw something black hanging from the bottom of a car. He stopped to investigate and found what turned out to be part of the dark fur coat Mrs. Mathews was wearing at the time she was killed. Joe Peck, a former prize fighter and owner of the car, was arrested and charged with the killings and I represented him. The fact that he did not stop after striking the two people made it a pretty tough case.

The accident had happened on a real dark night while the two were crossing in the middle of the block. There was no street light and they were wearing dark clothing. Joe said he did not see them until he had struck them and, because he had become so excited, he couldn't stop until he had gone about a half block. He looked back and saw people running toward the two on the ground and he said he was then afraid to go back. It was my contention at the trial that there was no negligence on his part.

Joe had been a prize fighter for many years and had been in more than five hundred fights. I argued that he was punch drunk, "back on his heels," that his brain and muscles did not have the coordination of an ordinary person. I put Ed Stein, Joe's manager, on the stand to prove Joe's condition. He testified that Joe's last fight was at New Orleans and, at that time, he decided Joe had better not fight anymore.

On cross-examination the Prosecuting Attorney asked Ed how he could tell that Joe's mind and muscles did not coordinate and work together. What nerves were affected? Ed replied, "When Joe's supposed to hit, he's way too late and when he's supposed to duck, he's way too late." This struck the jury just the right way and they returned a verdict of not guilty.

In another case I represented a man named Vanderporten who was charged with killing a woman by shooting her in the back of the head with a pistol. The evidence showed that the defendant, a married man, had become infatuated with another woman and, after going with her for some time, decided to divorce his wife and marry her. He and the woman were in a car which Vanderporten was driving on the way to his house to inform his wife of his decision. When the car came within about one hundred feet of his house, he changed his mind, stopped the car, and turned around in the middle of the block. There a scuffle took place and, after considerable argument while parked at the curb, the state contended that the defendant simply shot the woman in the back of the head.

For the defense, I contended that the woman had hold of Vanderporten's arm with her teeth, biting for all she was worth; that Vanderporten grabbed his pistol which was beside the seat and struck her with it, and that the gun went off accidentally. There was some difficulty showing just how the bullet hit her in the back of the head. This weakness was offset by the state in contending that the woman was pregnant by Vanderporten and that was what the trouble was really all about. But I was able to show that she had had a hysterectomy and he was acquitted. It was always my belief that Vanderporten did not shoot her at all, that she was shot by a third person (his wife) and that Vanderporten just took the blame. This acquittal was winning against the odds!

There was another case that attracted my attention, even though I did not represent anyone involved, but I had been in the army with Jack Howard, one of the principles.

There was a man from Hot Springs named Tom Slaughter who had been sent to the penitentiary. At that time (the early 1930s) the Arkansas Penitentiary was a very tough place, perhaps the toughest in the nation. Punishment was inflicted by whipping a convict with a very heavy leather strap. The pain was intense and it was said that it felt like being burned with a hot iron.

Not only was the strap very severe punishment, but the work was hard. There were about 20,000 acres of land planted mostly in cotton, worked by the convicts. The planting of the cotton in itself was not a big task. The land was prepared and planted by the use of mules and hand labor. But after the cotton came up, it had to be chopped out by hand with hoes, thinning the stand and getting rid of the grass. The long hours from daylight to dark made the work very tiring. Sometimes when the convicts were chopping cotton, perhaps two miles from headquarters and had been working about 12 hours, they would be compelled to trot back to the barracks to get there before it was too dark.

Incidentally, the barracks where the convicts were confined, were constructed of nothing but wood. But there were no escapes. The punishment by use of the strap was so great for an attempt to escape, that it was very seldom attempted. Three licks with the strap would cause excruciating pain, and there were cases of a convict having been hit as many as 75 licks with the strap.

Al Reed, who had been connected with the penitentiary system in one capacity or another and at one time was Superintendent, told me that if a convict was set free after serving only six months in the Arkansas Penitentiary, he would never come back; that during this first six month period, he thought that he could not make it, that he would surely die. But after serving a longer period of time, he found out that he could survive and thereafter was not nearly so afraid.

Finally, I believe it was in the 1970's, the matter got into Federal Court and there, the court held that the use of the strap was a violation of the Constitution of the United States. Not only that, but the court abolished other inhumane practises and practically took charge of how the prison should be operated.

When Tom Slaughter arrived at the "pen," he resisted the normal procedure of having his head clipped and this resulted in a severe shipping. The next day Slaughter told the warden, Dee Horton, who was a very brutal man, that he would not cause any more trouble, that he knew he had been wrong the day before. Horton replied that he knew that Slaughter would cause no more trouble and proceeded to give him another whipping. This was done by making the convict lie on the ground with another convict holding his legs down and still another convict sitting on his head.

A few weeks later Slaughter somehow got possession of a high-powered rifle used by a guard. He attempted to kill the warden, but missed and killed another prisoner instead. Slaughter was charged with first degree murder in the prisoner's death, convicted and sentenced to death.

While he was awaiting execution at the "Walls" in Little Rock where the electric chair was located, he managed to grab a guard and get his pistol. He made the guard open the cell door. Slaughter then released Jack Howard, who was also a prisoner at the Walls, and they both got in the warden's car and drove out the front gate.

They went west and when they came to a side road near Benton, Arkansas, they drove out to a place in the woods and Slaughter went to sleep. Howard then took the pistol and shot Slaughter in the head, killing him, after which he surrendered to local officers. Of course, Howard thought he would receive some consideration for killing Slaughter, and he did. He was released from prison a short time later.

I was in the army with a fellow named Higgenbotham and, about the time I started practicing law, he shot and killed his wife's brother in a cottonfield in Lonoke County. It was said the trouble came up over a venereal disease. Higgenbotham was charged with murder and tried at Lonoke. Tom Trimble, who later became a United States District Judge at Little Rock, represented Higgenbotham; and Bill Wagner, who later became the Circuit Judge at Lonoke, was the Prosecuting Attorney. Higgenbotham asked me to testify for him as a character witness and I agreed to do so.

At the trial I testified as to the time I had known Higgenbotham in the army, that he was of good character, and was a peaceful and law-abiding citizen. On cross-examination, Wagner asked me if I knew Higgenbotham had a veneral disease while he was in the army. I said, "No, I did not know that, but it would not have affected his reputation because so many others had it." Wagner asked me no further questions.

First and last, I tried all kinds of cases. An Italian shoemaker from Sicily named Scalisi who had his shop down the street from my office came to see me about getting a divorce. He spoke very little English, but I managed to get the information I needed. His wife lived in Sicily, not far from Palermo, and I notified her of the suit by registered mail.

In due time I received a letter from her lawyers at Palermo. The letter was in Italian and I got my friend, Father Fletcher, a Catholic priest who later became Bishop of Arkansas, to interpret it for me. In the letter the lawyers said that there was no objection to Scalisi getting the divorce. The last time anyone in Italy had heard of him was thirty years before when he had burned his house, with all of his children in it, and disappeared.

In yet another case, Morehead Smith, a Negro, shot at another Negro, missed him and hit a young white woman, Myrna Lawrence, who was on the other side of the street. She was the daughter of a policeman. The bullet hit her in the side and passed all the way through her body. Although she fully recovered, there was a good deal of bad feeling toward Smith for having shot a white woman, especially the daughter of a policeman. Smith was charged with assault with intent to kill and I defended him.

At the trial, after the state had introduced all of its evidence, I moved for a directed verdict on the grounds that to sustain the charge the defendant must have had the specific intent to kill the woman. The evidence,I said, showed just the contrary, that Smith didn't even know she was on the street. I had ample authority to sustain my motion and it was granted. The case against Smith was dismissed and there was a good deal of feeling against me for a while, but things soon blew over.

I defended another man who was charged with killing a patient at the Arkansas State Hospital for Nervous Diseases where the defendant was an attendant. The dead man's kin had come from the northern part of the state to claim the body which had already been placed in a coffin. According to the relatives, when they got home they discovered several broken bones in the body. They then made a complaint to the State Hospital and an investigation was made which found that the attendant had used force on the patient who had become completely unruly. As a result of this finding, murder charges were filed.

At the trial, I was able to show that the casket containing the body of the dead man had fallen out of the truck on the journey home. It had broken open, the body had rolled down a steep mountain and I maintained that the bones were broken at that time. The attendant was acquitted. In the course of preparing the case, I visited a veteran's hospital at Fort Logan H. Roots in North Little Rock. I received permission to view the facilities there for handling unruly patients with the purpose of comparing it with the very poor facilities at the Arkansas State Hospital at that time. I was in a large room at the government hospital when they brought in a patient who was just raving. I recognized him as a soldier who had served in France with the same company as I. Try as I could, I could not get him to recognize me.

The doctors in the government hospital made a diagnosis in another case I had. I represented a man in a claim for damages against a mining company where he was working when he received serious head injuries. A pulley had fallen down a mine shaft striking the man on the head. After the injuries had apparently healed, he had no feeling in his skin. He could be pricked with a needle from the top of his head to the bottom of his feet, anywhere on his body, and he could not feel any of it.

I had a conference with Dr. Samuel G. Boyce, the injured man's physician, and he was uncertain as to the diagnosis of the man's condition. Dr. Boyce conferred with the doctors at Fort Logan H. Roots which led to a diagnosis of "syringomyelia." He called me after the diagnosis had been made asking me to come to his office so that he could tell me all about the information he had just learned. It was obvious that he was very anxious to tell me about the diagnosis — he was just full of it. I arrived at his office at five o'clock and Dr. Boyce dismissed his office staff, locked the door, and began to tell me all about syringomyelia.

He had been talking for some time when his phone rang. I could tell he did not want to answer it, but he finally did so and began "yessing" the lady on the other end of the line. He'd say, "yes…, yes…, yes…, yes, that will be all right!" It was obvious that he wanted to end the conversation but the lady would not let him go. After a long pause, he said, "Yes, it'll be all right to put a hot poultice on it. Yes…, yes, it'll be all right to put a cold poultice on it. Hot poultice…, cold poultice— any kind of damn poultice!" and slammed down the phone. And this is what I remember when I think of this case. Oh, the mining company made a satisfactory settlement.

Unforeseen things sometimes happen during a trial. Sometimes it is tragic, sometimes it is funny, and sometimes it is a little of both.

Bob Rogers, my former partner, and I were representing a man charged with murder. The deceased man had been having an affair with the defendant's wife so the defendant simply put a pistol in his pocket, found the other man and killed him. From what the defendant told us, he had a fairly good case of self-defense.

We wanted the jury to know that the defendant had been in the army and had a good war record. We decided it would be best if these facts came out on cross-examination, rather than the defendant testifying to it on direct examination. We told him that we weren't going to ask him anything about his war record when we questioned him, but that the first time he had a chance to mention it on cross-examination, to do so.

After we finished the direct examination, Henry Donham, the Prosecuting Attorney and a great lawyer, took the man on cross- examination and just looked at him for a short time. Finally, with a faint smile on his face and in a rather kind tone of voice, he asked, "Why did you kill that man?" The defendant straightened up in his chair, squared his shoulders and, in a firm tone of voice, said, "Because he broke up my home and I killed him like any other ex-serviceman would have done." Henry said, "That's all. No further questions," his original contention that there was no justification for the killing having just been proven and the man was convicted of manslaughter.

In the heart of the great depression of the 1930's, I bought a house on Park Hill from an insurance company that had foreclosed on it. I knew the man who had owned the place and we had previously talked of the matter.

A few months after moving in, the telephone rang early one morning. The caller said that I owed some money to the man who had been foreclosed on and, if I didn't pay, he was going to kill me. He then hung up and it made me real mad.

I got in touch with the operator right quick and found out that the call had come from Hot Springs. I suspected that it was the former owner himself who had done the calling. The Chief of Detectives at Hot Springs was Swede Watkins, a real good friend of mine and I called him immediately. I told him what had happened, and asked him to check with people in the vicinity of prominently located pay phones to try to get a description of the man who made the call.

Swede went to work and in about two hours he called me back at my office with a description of a man who had made a call from the Pullman Hotel; a large man about six feet tall, freckled face and about 35 years of age. The description fit the former owner of my house. He ran a used car lot just about four blocks from my office in Little Rock so I called him there and told him about the call I had received that morning. I also told him that I thought he had made the call. He admitted to doing so and said that he meant what he had said. I told him to meet me at Second and Spring Street, which was halfway between my office and his used car lot, and that he could commence his killing. He said he'd do just that.

It was cold and I put on my overcoat and put my pistol in the side pocket where I could hold it in my hand. I walked down to Second and Spring, took up a good position, and waited. The man never did snow up and that ended the matter. About a year later he was indicted in Federal Court charged with having bought a stolen car being transported in interstate commerce and he retained me to defend him. I did and he was acquitted.

In the old days many kinds of trickery and chicanery were sometimes used in the trial of lawsuits, especially in criminal cases. Even the fixing of juries was not uncommon and two times in my career I was sure that juries were fixed against me; once, by government authorities in a Federal Court when I was representing the defendant, and again, in State Court where I was prosecuting a person for murder.

Dr. Rowland was a friend of mine who was the Superintendent of the Arkansas State Hospital for Nervous Diseases. At the time he told me the following story which took place in the southern part of the state. He related that in the early 1900's a friend of his, a prominent man, was charged with murder. In addition to a local lawyer, Jeff Davis - a well-known lawyer, one time governor of Arkansas and later a United States Senator, was also representing him.

The man's trial came on the docket in November. The defense considered the trial judge, George Hayes - later governor of Arkansas, and the jury to be unfavorable. But both would be replaced in the new year at the start of the new term, so the defense made every effort to get the case continued. They alleged that the defendant was sick and unable to stand trial. But the trial judge was determined that the case would be tried while he was still in office. He refused to grant the continuance and proceeded with the selection of the jury.

Dr. Rowland told me that he took a hypodermic syringe and loaded it with something that would knock out the defendant. During the jury selection, he sat down next to the defendant and shot him into his leg through his pants, injecting the knockout substance. In just a little bit, the drug took effect and the defendant passed out. He just fell over unconscious on the table right there in the courtroom as Jeff Davis jumped to his feet and began to shout, "Judicial murder! Judicial murder!" Judge Hayes, fearing that perhaps the man had died, immediately ordered the continuance. Later, when the man was tried before another judge and jury, he was acquitted.

And, of course, trickery and chicanery aren't confined to the courtroom. Horse trading is another profession known to use one or the other or both upon occasion.

I loved horses all my life and most of the time I have owned some. I have traded quite a few and I don't suppose a friend of mine, Ned Smith, who lived west of Little Rock, ever did anything else. One time on the way to a horse sale, he told me of some of his experiences and some of those of his father, who was a horse trader before him.

In the old days, horse traders would start out the year with a string of horses, the families riding in wagons, and the horses coming along behind. They would trade horses anywhere on the road or they would stop near a town and stay a few days. Horse traders always had a "snide," a horse that appeared to be real good when, in fact, it had something real bad wrong with it. Good snides were few and far between.

Ned told me that his father had a "snide" that looked and acted real good when he had a saddle on, but actually the horse was real swayback. He would make the horse's back look smooth by using sacks and other material before saddling the horse, which would then appear to be okay.

After the trade was made, his father would remove the saddle and, at that point, everything would still appear to be allright with the saddle blanket still in place. Then he would start removing the blankets and the other padding. He would take these things off one at a time very slowly, and of course, the man who had traded for the horse would be getting sicker and sicker all the time. Finally Smith would reach the last thing he had used to cover up the swayback — a great big cow's liver! By that time, the man who had bought the horse was willing to trade back for anything, usually a very cheap watch.

But sometimes the other party to the trade realized what had happened and would keep the "snide." The horse trader would then have to make a real good deal to get his "snide" back and the farmer usually came out on the good end of the trade in this deal.

Ed MacDonald, who had been Grant County Sheriff, was elected Secretary of State where he served two terms and then ran for governor. His opponent in the gubernatorial race was Carl Bailey, who had been Prosecuting Attorney at Little Rock and later, Attorney General. Bailey won the governor's race by only a small margin over MacDonald. Fred Donham, Bailey's Chief Deputy Prosecuting Attorney, was then elected prosecuting Attorney.

When MacDonald was Secretary of State, he was in charge of the maintenance of the State Capitol Building. Not long after Bailey took office as Governor and Donham took office as Prosecuting Attorney, MacDonald was indicted on charges of having bought unneeded janitorial supplies, having paid an excessive price for these supplies, and receiving a kickback from the supplier. He retained me to defend him.

The case was set for trial at an early date and our defense was that the charges against MacDonald were trumped up, not made of the whole cloth, but for the purpose of politically destroying him. Due to the closeness of the vote in the gubernatorial election, Bailey had won by only a majority of 3,000 votes, MacDonald was potentially a dangerous opponent for Bailey in the next election. The trial was quite lengthy and the State put ninety-two witnesses on the stand, including the owner of the janitorial supply house at Memphis from whom MacDonald had purchased the state supplies though the man did not testify to one thing that would hurt MacDonald.

When the Prosecuting Attorney announced that the State closed its case, I announced that the defense also closed its case. We had not put one witness on the stand. I never did like to put a defendant on the stand unless it was absolutely necessary, as usually he is under great pressure and, hence, nervous and his testimony is looked upon with suspicion by the jury. After the closing arguments and instructions from the court, the jury retired to deliberate MacDonald's guilt or innocence. But it never did reach a verdict and the hung jury was discharged by the court.

The case was set for retrial. In the meantime, the owner of the janitorial supply house was tried for defrauding the state, convicted, and sent to the Arkansas penitentiary. A few days before MacDonald's second trial, I learned that the State was again going to use the convicted man as a witness. I realized the State would not use him unless he had agreed to change his testimony, as his original testimony had not hurt MacDonald at the first trial.

The governor had full charge at the pentitentiary, having authority to appoint and remove the warden at will. Bailey had done this at the time he became Governor, removing Tom Cogbill who had been there for some time, and appointing another man.

In those days the principal method of punishment at the Arkansas penitentiary was "the strap". It was made of heavy leather about five feet long, two and a half inches wide, a quarter-inch thick and bolted to a wooden handle a foot and a half long. The convict to be punished was made to lie on his stomach and a convict would sit on his head, and another on his feet, and he would be whipped on the buttocks with the strap. I had it on good authority that the pain was terrible — as mentioned in the Slaughter incident.

Tom Cogbill was a friend of mine and I went to see him. He had brought one of the straps away with him when he left the penitentiary and I borrowed it from him, practicing with the strap until I could actually break a piece of concrete with it. If used just right, the strap sounded like a big gun going off.

The day the owner of the supply house was to testify, I folded the strap, placed it in a big paper bag, and gave it to a young lawyer and friend of mine, Dave Witt, to take into the courtroom. He sat with the spectators and when I gave him the signal, he was to bring the bag to me at the counsel table.

When the State put the man who was now serving his term in the penitentiary on the stand, he testified to just the reverse of what he had said in the first trial. He now stated that MacDonald had bought a whole lot more supplies than were needed, that an exorbitant price had been paid for them, and that he had given back to MacDonald part of the money the State had paid for the supplies. If the jury believed what the man said, MacDonald was ruined, there was sure to be a conviction.

I had a transcript of the first trial and on cross-examination, I made the witness admit that he had changed his testimony. I asked him why and he said he had "just decided to tell the truth." With that, I gave the signal to Dave Witt to bring the paper bag to me. I pulled the strap out of the bag by the handle and let the leather part fall full length. The witness turned deathly white! I asked him if he knew what the strap was and he said he did. Then I demanded to know if it was the reason he had changed his testimony and I hit the floor with the strap using all my strength — it sounded like a cannon!

The whole courtroom was thrown into an uproar and the judge started hollering to the sheriff to take the strap away from me. Meanwhile, I was backing up, striking the floor with the strap. Sheriff Branch was a short man and I managed to hold him off with one hand while still striking the floor, but he finally got it away from me. After the commotion died down, I got the witness to admit that he had seen it used in the pen, but he continued to deny that he himself had been whipped. Nevertheless, I had made my point.

The State again used a large number of witnesses. I, again, used none and, again, there was a hung jury. The court let the jury stay out three days and three nights, but they could not reach a verdict. They spent the biggest part of their time arguing about the strap. We later learned that the vote was six to six on the first ballot and remained that way for the entire time. The case was never tried again.

The State had used ninety-two witnesses, we used none — this was winning against the odds!

Chapter XIV

Grace

I represented Grace Goldstein in a case in Federal court in Little Rock and while she was in jail, she told me her life story. Grace was a nice looking woman although not beautiful. She was of medium height and weighed about 130 pounds; had fair skin and long, light brown hair that she usually wore done up on her head. She was intelligent and dressed conservatively. Her overall appearance was sexy but she did not look like what the ordinary person might think a whore would look like.

Grace told me she was born out in the country in Texas and lived there until she was about seventeen years old when she went to Dallas where she got a job in a millinery shop making ladies' hats. After working at the shop a while, one of the other women there got her to go along on a double date. It soon turned out that this woman was dating men for money in exchange for sex. Grace followed suit and collected a pretty good fee from her date. She told me she was paid more for that date than for a week in the millinery shop.

From then on Grace dated men for money, soon quitting her job at the millinery shop, and began doing business as a full-time prostitute. She then moved to New Orleans where she worked in several houses of prostitution.

Eventually, a man who was seeing her often, prevailed upon her to leave the whorehouse. He set her up in a swanky apartment along with giving her a good deal of money. She was supposed to be seeing just him and no one else, but it wasn't long before she met another man who also wanted to set her up. So she got another apartment right across the hall from the first one.

Neither of the men could see her very often and it was no trouble for her to arrange things so they would never be there at the same time. She would move pictures and trinkets and other little things they would recognize from one apartment to the other, depending on which one was there. One of the men owned a string of department stores and is still a nationally known figure, although deceased. Grace lived this way for quite a while and accumulated some money. After both men dropped her, she decided to move to Hot Springs, Arkansas, and open a whorehouse of her own.

At that time, Hot Springs was wide open with casino-type gambling as well as whorehouses, although all of it was illegal. The law was simply not enforced. Grace told me her real name was Jewel Laverne Grayson. But on the way to Hot Springs, she decided to change it to Grace Goldstein as she had always heard that Jews were lucky. She opened an elaborate house and all the whores who came to Hot Springs wanted to work there. She had the pick of the crop and the best-looking because they could make more money in her house, and she got the men who could spend the most money because she had the best-looking women.

Alvin Karpis and his gang had robbed the mails of two million dollars in Illinois. Karpis had made arrangements with John Stover, a young fellow who owned and ran a flying service at Hot Springs, to pick him up and fly him, along with several large suitcases, back to Hot Springs. To Stover it was just another trip. The rest of the gang got there by various means. When they all met again, they rented a house on one of the three large lakes near town.

Karpis and his gang started patronizing Grace's house and Karpis took up with Grace, herself, as his woman. Another of the gang took up with one of Grace's girls named Connie. During this whole time, Karpis had with him a very conspicuous, large, black Great Dane dog. Why in the world he would attract attention to himself in this manner, no one knows. But he also made himself conspicuous in the manner he spent money. He and Grace would drive into a "drive-in" restaurant, order a Coca Cola which then cost a nickel, and tell the carhop to keep the change from a ten-dollar bill . This was in the thirties when a ten- dollar bill was a lot of money, about a week's wages for a waitress. At one point Grace and Karpis took a trip to Florida and while there, bought a little alligator about twelve or fourteen inches long. When they returned to Hot Springs, they simply put it in the bathtub at the house the gang had rented out at the lake.

The Federal Bureau of Investigation finally located the gang and one day a large number of agents got off the plane at Little Rock. When they got to Hot Springs, Grace learned of them and undertook to warn the gang out at the lake. Realizing that anyone leaving her house would be followed by the agents, she devised a plan to elude them.

She knew how to go through the surrounding buildings to get to her car, making it difficult for anyone to immediately follow. So she had Connie walk down the street and go through the front door of a hotel and right out the back door where Grace was waiting in her car. The plan worked okay and they got to the lake without being followed where the gang was holed up. The gang packed immediately, got into their cars, and Grace led them to a back-country road which enabled them to get away undetected.

After they got away, Grace started back to Hot Springs. But she then remembered the little alligator in the bathtub. So she turned around, went back, got the alligator out of the tub and took it down to the lake where she turned it loose. She then drove back to Hot Springs, this time barely escaping the arrival of the FBI. The agents, thinking the gang was still inside the house, shot the house full of bullet holes causing the government to pay the owner of the house considerable damages.

The Karpis gang was later arrested at New Orleans. It is my understanding that Karpis was personally arrested by J. Edgar Hoover who, up to that date, had never made an arrest and had been taunted for not having done so. The arrest of Karpis by Hoover had been planned in a foolproof manner so there would be no mishap. FBI agents had Karpis well located and learned his usual route of travel around the city. The agents blocked Karpis' car at an intersection and Hoover, standing on the curb waiting for this to happen, ran up to the car, put a pistol to his head, and said. "Alvin Karpis, you are under arrest." I don't know about the truthfulness of this story, but it is what I heard.

They were tried, convicted, and given long sentences in the Federal Penitentiary with Karpis serving about twenty-five years in Alcatraz. Indicted in Federal Court in Little Rock on charges of conspiracy in connection with the mail robbery were: Wakeland - the Chief of Police in Hot Springs; Akers - the Chief of Detectives; John Stover - the pilot who flew Karpis to Hot Springs; and Grace. They were all tried at the same time and I initially represented Stover.

When the government had rested its case against Stover, I moved for a directed verdict on the grounds that there was no evidence to show he had been involved in any conspiracy. We retired to the judge's chambers and after considerable argument with the government attorney stoutly opposing my motion, the court granted it and the case against Stover was dismissed.

A recess was called and during that time Grace Goldstein retained me to continue in the case on her behalf. Jim Campbell, who was representing Grace, welcomed me into her case. But nevertheless, the three remaining defendants, Wakeland, Ackers and Grace were convicted as charged.

Grace had also been indicted on a charge of transporting a female in interstate commerce for immoral purposes. A few days after the first trial, she was tried on this charge and I defended her. But she was again convicted. She was sent to a federal women's reformatory for a short time in Virginia and I never saw her again.

Chapter XV

The Prosecuting Years

In 1940 I had decided to run for Prosecuting Attorney for the Sixth Judicial District of Arkansas, which included Pulaski County where Little Rock is located. I was elected and took office the first day of January, 1941. On the following December 7th, the Japanese attacked Pearl Harbor and the next day, December 8th, we declared war on Japan.

I was 42 years of age at the time, and I wanted to go into the army. I had a Commission as an officer in the Reserve Corps., but in the prevailing circumstances, I could not see my way clear to go. I had a wife, two children and no money - and after considering the matter for some time, I decided that I had better stay with my job of Prosecuting Attorney.

During the war, a large number of soldiers, perhaps 100,000, were stationed at Camp Robinson, right north of Little Rock. And of course, there were instances in which a soldier would get into trouble. But I never prosecuted one of them. It was our policy to turn them over to the military authorities.

On one occasion, however, I did defend a soldier at a general court martial. One day a young woman came to my office and told me that she was the wife of a Corporal who was stationed at Camp Robinson. He was charged with striking an officer and was in prison at the camp. He was to be tried by a general court martial, she said, and asked me to defend him. I told her I would look into the matter. As a Prosecuting Attorney, I would not defend a person in a federal court, but a court martial was another matter.

I went to see the officer who had been appointed to defend the soldier and he had no objection to my entering the case, in fact he urged me to do so. I then went to the Major General of the camp, explained the situation to him, and asked if there would be any objection to my representing the accused. He said I would be more than welcome to appear in the case.

Next, I went to see the defendant in the guardhouse and he told me his version of what had happened. Then I looked up the army rules and regulations concerning such violations and came to the conclusion that the Corporal was not guilty. When his wife returned to my office, I told her I would take the case.

The soldier told me he was driving his automobile down Main Street and, at the corner of Fifth and Main, he had a near collision with another automobile. One of the occupants of the other car jumped out and ran over to the Corporal's car which was stopped at the intersection. He stepped up on the running board and, at that time, the Corporal hit him squarely in the face, knocking him loose from the automobile. There were MP's nearby and the Corporal was arrested then and there on the charge of striking an officer. It turned out that the man he hit was a Major and was the executive officer of Camp Robinson. The soldier told me that he didn't know it was an officer that had jumped on the side of his car and that he would never strike an officer. He thought it was just another soldier looking for trouble.

I immediately began work on the case. I found out the defendant had a splendid war record and had served in more than one foreign country. At Camp Robinson I was able to locate some officers with whom he had served and they all stated that he was a good soldier, had a good reputation, and was not the kind of man who would strike an officer. And they all agreed to testify in his behalf.

The case was heard by a military court of five officers and lasted about two days. The court was not long in returning a verdict of not guilty.

I served as prosecuting Attorney for six years, being elected to two more terms. I had several deputy prosecutors and handled hundreds of cases during that time, but I will only mention some of the unusual ones that I prosecuted myself. They were mostly murder and rape cases.

In the early 1940's the buildings at the Arkansas State Hospital for Nervous Diseases were very old and there were no modern facilities for handling unruly patients. When I was in private practice I defended several people on charges of killings that took place there and I also prosecuted several murder cases from there as Prosecuting Attorney. I remember one particularly gruesome case in which a patient had been scalded to death. Two attendants were charged with the killing. They claimed it was accidental but I was convinced otherwise and they were convicted of second-degree murder.

Another case occurred about the same time in which one patient killed another patient. They both occupied the same room and the one who did the killing worked for a long time, using just his hands, to loosen the wooden facing on the window frame so he could get to the heavy weights which allowed the window to be raised and lowered. He was finally able to remove one of the weights and, while his roommate slept, hit him in the head with it. It was perfectly clear the man who did the killing was totally insane and no charge was made.

On a Monday morning the parents of a sixteen-year-old Negro girl brought her to my office and told me she had been raped the previous day by two white men. I questioned the girl in great detail and came to the conclusion she was telling the truth. She told me she had been to church and, after leaving, she was crossing the street about a block away when a police car stopped and the policeman told her to get into the car. The policeman and a cab driver, who was also in the car, took her to the edge of town and parking on some vacant property near a railroad, both men raped her.

I immediately got in touch with the Chief of Police and informed him of what I had been told. The girl had given me a good description of the policeman and it was not long until he was located and confronted with the charge. He identified the other man as a local cab driver and admitted that they both had sex with the girl, but stated it was a mutual proposition with no rape involved. The two men were arrested and, after talking to both of them, I was still of the opinion that the girl was telling the truth. They were both charged with rape and I personally prosecuted the case.

In Arkansas at that time there were three possible outcomes from a guilty verdict in a rape indictment. If the jury returned the verdict of guilty of rape as charged in the indictment, the defendant received the death penalty. Or, the jury could add to fix the penalty at life imprisonment. And there was another possibility; the jury could return yet a third guilty verdict by saying, "We, the jury, find the defendant guilty of assault with intent to rape," and fix the penalty at not more than twenty-one years in the penitentiary.

The policeman and the cab driver testified that they had stopped the police car to let the girl cross the street but that she walked up to the car and began a conversation with them. The conversation, they both said, resulted in her agreeing to have sex with them and they went out to the place where the acts were committed. The girl testified that the officer stopped the car and told her to get in and that she hadn't said anything.

I was thoroughly convinced that the men were guilty and tried the case as hard as I could. I asked the jury to return a verdict of guilty of rape as charged in the indictment, which would have carried the death penalty. But the jury returned a verdict of assault with intent to rape, with the men still getting stiff sentences.

The old saying "You can never tell what a jury is going to do" is also well illustrated by the following case. A Negro was arrested and confessed to killing a white man by knocking out his brains with a blunt instrument. When the officer talked with me about the case, they had not yet found the weapon. The defendant had told them that he had hit the man in the back of the head with a rock, and I said, "Well, let's go get the rock."

In many cases a person committing a violent crime will try to do away with the weapon. He will tell all about the circumstances of the crime, but not what he did with the weapon. An officer and I took the defendant to the scene of the crime and had him look for the rock he claimed he had used to kill the white man. As suspected, he could not find it and finally confessed to using the blunt end of an ax which he had then thrown into a creek not far from there. The creek was only about two feet deep and we saw the ax handle sticking out of the water and recovered it.

From my investigation of the case I concluded that the Negro man had committed the killing because he and the white man were having sex with the same Negro woman and the crime was committed out of jealousy. It was a deliberate, cold-blooded crime, having all the elements of first-degree murder. But I did not believe that the defendant should be convicted of first-degree murder even though he had slipped up behind the deceased and knocked his brains out with an ax.

In the trial of the case, I was afraid that the jury would return a verdict of first-degree murder with the death penalty. I prosecuted the case in the best light I could for the defendant and I was thinking that a twenty-one year sentence for second- degree murder would be about right. But, to my surprise, the jury returned the verdict of voluntary manslaughter, fixing the penalty at a few years in the penitentiary, which was all right with me.

During my six years as Prosecuting Attorney, there was only one case in which there was a verdict of not guilty in a case tried by me. This was the case of an eighteen-year-old boy who was charged with murdering his mother. His acquittal was due, in large measure, to an erroneous ruling by the trial court on the exclusion of some very important evidence.

I was incensed by the ruling of the court and after the not-guilty verdict, I decided to appeal the matter to the State Supreme Court. The youth could not be put on trial again after he had been found not guilty because that would be putting the defendant in jeopardy twice for the same offense. Never the less, I wanted the Supreme Court to pass on the point of the erroneous ruling because of several other cases that were pending. The high court found in my favor and that was the end of the matter.

About that time, a little girl's body was found in a wooded area near the western city limits of Little Rock. She was about eleven years old and had been dead about a week. After she was identified, it was found that she had been reported missing by the family. The autopsy showed she had been raped and then strangled to death.

Her family said she had failed to come home after school one afternoon and, upon questioning children at her school, officers found one girl who remembered seeing the deceased go off with a man. The girl said she would recognize him, so officers took her riding up and down the main streets of Little Rock for quite a while and finally she pointed out a man she said was the one and he was arrested. This twelve-year-old girl picked him out of hundreds of people that day and she was positive of her identification of him as the one she saw leaving the school with the murdered girl. Furthermore, it turned out that he was the murdered girl's uncle!

The man was questioned and he could give no satisfactory account of his whereabouts at the time the girl disappeared. Officers also found other witnesses who identified the man as having been seen with the little girl. And even his next door neighbor saw him sitting under a tree across the street from the school before it let out that afternoon. Finally, the man admitted to the officers that he had committed the crime and he was charged with murder in the first degree.

At the trial I told the jury in my opening statement that the man had confessed to the crime. In the course of the trial, when I attempted to introduce the confession into evidence, the attorney for the defendant objected on the grounds that the confession was not voluntary. We went into the judge's chambers to argue the point. There the defense attorney introduced pretty convincing evidence that the confession had been obtained by the officers with third-degree methods. During a recess for lunch, I had an opportunity to talk with the officers who had obtained the alleged voluntary confessions and from this talk I was convinced it indeed had been wrongfully obtained. When we went back to the judge's chambers after lunch, I told the court that I would not attempt to rebut the evidence, that the confession was involuntary, and that I would not attempt to introduce the confession as evidence.

We proceeded with the trial and, although I did not use the confession, I failed to withdraw from the jury my remarks in my opening statement to the effect that there had been a confession. The defendant was convicted of first-degree murder as charged in the indictment and, as in a murder indictment, this carried the death penalty. On defendant's appeal to the State Supreme court, the Court held that there was prejudicial error in my failure to withdraw from the jury the statement regarding the confession. The case was reversed and set for retrial which again resulted in a verdict of guilty, but with a sentence of life imprisonment. On a subsequent appeal by the defendant, this verdict was afirmed. During the second trial I made no mention of any confession and no attempt was made to introduce it into evidence.

I never prosecuted a case in which I did not sincerely believe that the defendant was guilty and should be convicted. This applies to cases in which a person may have been technically guilty of violation of the law, but as I saw things, according to everything that was just, fair and right, the defendant should not be punished, so I simply did not prosecute. In one instance, the grand jury indicted a man against my advice and, while the jury was still in session, I simply dismissed the case in circuit court. There was no further attempt made to obtain an indictment.

In another case, a very unusual circumstance occurred where a woman killed her husband. The man had been mistreating his wife for a long time, getting drunk, coming home, and beating her up. His mistreatment of her grew worse as time passed.

One day when he came home drunk and beat on her, she got away from him and ran next door where she obtained a pistol. She and the lady of the house locked the front door, but it wasn't long before the drunken husband was banging on the door trying to get into the house.

When it looked like he might break down the door, his terrified wife just shot through it. The man must have had his chest right against the door at the time because the bullet penetrated the door and struck him in the heart. His blood squirted back through the bullet-hole in the door and ran down the inside. There was no question of what had happened; the evidence was there to speak for itself. The woman might have been technically guilty of violating the law, but I never charged her and nothing was ever done about the incident.

In another case, the dairymen who supplied the Little Rock stores with milk were demanding an increase in price. The stores refused and the dairymen went on strike. It was in the forties and one dairyman named Brown, refused to join the others and continued to supply his customers. Those on strike threatened him on several occasions, but he still continued to deliver milk.

The strikers had a meeting and agreed that they would stop Brown the following morning and try to prevail upon him not to deliver any more milk in Little Rock. They decided that if he failed to meet their demands, they would turn over his truck and destroy his load of milk. They congregated on the road they knew Brown would be using to get to Little Rock.

As Brown came down the road he saw them. He stopped about one hundred yards from them and started backing up in anticipation of what the strikers had in mind. A teen-age boy was in the truck with him acting as his helper. As Brown began to back up his truck the men started running after him and a shot was fired from the truck killing one of the strikers.

An investigation of the incident was undertaken immediately and Brown surrendered saying he fired the shot that killed the other dairyman. He did so, he said, because they were gaining on him and he was afraid of what they would do if they caught him.

I concluded that the men who tried to stop Brown were the ones who had committed the crime in assembling to violate the law and that Brown had acted in self-defense. Several of the group involved came to my office and demanded that Brown be prosecuted to the full extent of the law for the killing of their friend. My response was that they had all better go and get the best lawyer they could because I was going to have every one of them indicted, adding that I was not going to ask for an indictment of Brown.

I assembled the grand jury and presented the entire matter to that body with the result I wanted,an indictment against the dairymen. But the case against them dragged on, was never tried, and was finally dismissed.

Fifteen years later, after I had been on the Supreme Court for a while, the phone rang rather late one night. A man asked if I remembered the Brown case and I told him I remembered it well. He said he was the teen-ager who was in the truck with Brown on the morning of the trouble and that he was the one who fired the shot into the group of pursuing dairymen. Brown had told him to keep quiet, that he would take the blame.

The man said the thing had been on his mind all these years and it had finally gotten to the point that he had to tell someone about it. His conscience would never be clear, he told me, if he didn't tell someone and that is why he called me. He asked what he should do and I told him to go on about his business, that it had been decided that Brown was not at fault. And, that since he had stood in Browns shoes, his position in the matter was the same. He said he was greatly relieved and I never heard any more about the case.

While Prosecuting Attorney, I had another similar case. There were several cottonseed oil mills at Little Rock. All but a few of the workers at the Southern Cottonseed Oil Company, a large operation, went on a strike and it lasted quite a while. The strikers even put up a tent which served as their headquarters not far from the entrance of the mill. And one day the strikers decided they would send a group to the mill entrance to stop the five who were still working, and try to prevail on them to join the strike. If the five could not be persuaded, they would be beaten up.

As planned, a group of the strikers congregated across the street from the mill entrance to wait for the five workers when they got off. When they attempted to stop the first worker that left the mill that evening, he refused and continued to walk up the street. He hadn't gone very far when one of the strikers ran after him so he started to run also. The striker caught up with him, but when the worker turned, he had a knife in his hand and stabbed the attacking striker, killing him. The man was arrested.

After the investigation I came to the conclusion that the worker had acted in self-defense and he was not prosecuted; and that the strikers were guilty of unlawful assembly as they had gathered to beat up the workers, much the same as in the case of the striking dairymen.

Five of the strikers were charged with unlawful assembly and, in this case, were convicted. The case was appealed to the United States Supreme Court, but the convictions were upheld.

One real bad case I had to prosecute was that of a Negro who was charged with raping a white woman. East of North Little Rock there was a lumbermill near a railroad crossing. The mill was on the north side of the tracks and, not far away on the south side of the tracks, a couple lived in a one-room shack. The man was elderly but his wife was quite young and pretty.

One evening after the mill closed down, a Negro opened the door to the shack, walked in, and closed the door behind him. In his hand was a gun, a sawed-off single-barrel twelve-gauge shotgun with the stock also sawed off, making of it a weapon to be handled just like a pistol. Once inside the shack, the Negro started slapping the couple around and then made the old man sit in a chair at the point of the gun in full view of the raping of his wife.

After the Negro left, the couple notified the police who began work immediately on the case. The two were able to give a good description of the rapist to the officers who started looking over all the personnel at the mill. In a few days they found a man who fit the description exactly. He was arrested, taken before the injured parties, and was positively identified.

A search of the mill also produced the gun which was well-described by the couple. It was found hidden near where the accused worked in the mill. Later on I introduced the gun into evidence in court and it was one of the most vicious-looking weapons I have ever seen. At a few feet it could blow a hole through a person that you could put your fist through. There was no doubt as to the guilt of the accused. He was found guilty of rape as charged in the indictment and went to the electric chair.

One of the most serious cases I had to deal with during my years as Prosecuting Attorney was the one of a man named Hall. He was a handsome, well-built man in his late twenties,with dark red hair and a nice smile, but one of the most deadly men with whom I have ever been in contact.

At the time I became aware of him, he was a taxi driver in Little Rock. Hall had borrowed a personal car of another taxi driver and returned it after two or three days at which time the owner of the car became suspicious that he had used it in the commission of some kind of crime. The man told his suspicions to his mother who, in turn, called the State Police who, in their turn, called the Little Rock Police Department.

Hall was known to the Little Rock Police Department as his wife had disappeared the previous year. He had been picked up for questioning but had denied any knowledge of her whereabouts or what had happened to her. He told the police that he and his wife had been to a dance where they had been drinking. When they returned home he laid down across the bed and immediately went to sleep and that, when he awoke, his wife was gone. He said he had never heard from her again and that is as far as the matter went.

When the police learned of the suspicions of the taxi driver who loaned his car to Hall, they picked up Hall and took him to headquarters where he was questioned and searched. The police had no knowledge of any specific crime he might have committed and Hall denied being guilty of any crime. In searching him, the police found a receipt for a package he had mailed from Camden, Arkansas, to a girl in Little Rock. The police recovered the package from the young woman and discovered it contained articles taken from a man found murdered near Camden.

Now the police really went to work. In a search of Hall's room, they found five hundred rounds of .45 automatic ammunition and articles subsequently identified as having been taken from other murdered people. There were four unsolved murders in the state in the previous two months, all with a similar pattern, and property belonging to each of the four was found in Hall's room. Each of the victims had been shot in the back of the head with a .45 and all of the killings had been committed in a wooded area about one hundred yards from a major highway.

When confronted with the evidence, Hall admitted he had killed all four people. Then he said, "Well, I know you think I killed my wife. You questioned me about it a year ago and I did kill her." Hall said they had been to a dance but that when they got home, he killed her by breaking her neck, placed her body in a car, and drove up the river road west of Little Rock with the idea of dumping the body in the Arkansas River. The closest he could get to the river was still a quarter of a mile away and he tried to carry his wife's body through the strip of woods. He got tired, dropped the body, and just left it there. Ironically, he was on land I leased from the city and I had horses and cattle there.

Sure enough, his wife's scattered remains were found at the place he pointed out to officials. Her father and mother were able to identify her by parts of clothing and her skull which contained the upper teeth. She had unusually long eye teeth as did her father. Hall was indicted at Little Rock for murder in the first degree in the killing of his wife. It was my personal feeling that he killed her because a short time before, they had been on a trip to Oregon and she was a witness to a killing he had committed there.

Prosecuting Attorneys in the other districts where he had committed killings were notified of the findings and Hall was indicted for murder in all of those districts as well. All the prosecuting attorneys involved met at my office in Little Rock to decide where he would first be tried with the result that I would try him for the murder of his wife.

Hall's plan for robbing and murdering his victims was simple but effective and depended a great deal on his clean-cut looks and good clothes. He would walk out of town on a main highway where he would have no trouble hitching a ride, always in a car with out-of-state plates. He would ride with the driver of the car until they reached a place where the highway went through a lonely, wooded area. He would then pull his .45, tell the driver it was a holdup, and make him stop. He would march the driver off into the woods a distance of about one hundred yards and shoot him in the back of the head, taking any valuables from the victim. He would drive the victim's car to the next town, park it on one of the side streets, take anything else of value, and walk out of town where he would hitch another ride.

Since the automobile he had just parked was from another state, it was not likely anyone would recognize it, and it might stay there for several days before any investigation was made. The body of the murdered person might never be found. In any event, by the time any investigation would be started, Hall would be hundreds of miles away.

After he was indicted for the five murders, officials made an extensive investigation and found thirty-eight murders in the western part of the United States which they concluded Hall had committed. Two of these were in Kansas where a doctor and a young soldier were killed. Apparently the doctor picked up Hall and before Hall could murder him, also picked up the young soldier and Hall solved the problem by killing them both. The soldier was going home to North Carolina on furlough and his mother and father attended Hall's trial in Little Rock.

Hall obtained a lawyer and entered a plea of not guilty by reason of insanity. His father testified for him, but his mother would not and it was thought that he had even murdered his brother. The two had left Arkansas on a trip to the West and his brother was never heard of again. Hall's insanity plea did not prevail. The jury found him guilty of murder in the first degree as charged in the indictment. He was executed in the electric chair.

Chapter XVI

Back to Private Practice

I decided to run for a fourth term as Prosecuting Attorney, but this was a mistake. No other prosecutor had ever been elected for more than two terms and I had already been elected to three. My opponent was Edwin Dunaway, a handsome young lawyer who had just returned from the navy where he had served as an officer. His father, a lawyer of outstanding ability, had already served as prosecuting attorney several years previously.

After a hard campaign, I was defeated and returned to the private practice of law. One of my first cases was the defense of a man named Hunt, in a divorce case. Frances Holtzendorff, a young woman lawyer, was representing his wife.

One night just after supper, I was called on the phone and told that my client was in jail and that I had better come down there just as soon as I could. At police headquarters, which was located next to the city jail, I learned that Hunt had killed his wife and the man she was with. I talked with Hunt for a while and he asked me to represent him in this matter.

I began working on the case at once, first going to the undertaker's where the dead woman's body was located as I wanted to see the position of the bullet holes. The nude body had been cleaned up and was on a table, but the bullet wounds were perfectly apparent. Hunt had used a .45 automatic, a large caliber weapon and some of the bullets had gone clear through her. It looked to me like she was shot all over. I had seen many other bullet riddled bodies in my lifetime, but I had never seen one shot up as bad as this one. I never saw the man's body as he was at another undertakers.

I located the automobile in which the two were seated at the time they were killed. I found bullet holes in the upholstery and also found the remains of a lunch the two had been eating. Hunt's wife and the man were shot a total of eleven times. A fully loaded .45 Colt automatic holds seven rounds of ammunition. So in order to shoot eleven times, Hunt had to eject the empty clip and insert a new one.

This was a really tough case. The double killing took place late in the day, although it was not yet dark, and the car was parked on a side street about a half mile from where the Hunts lived. The man and woman in the car were not armed and Hunt had shot them eleven times at point blank range.

Hunt gave this version of what happened. Saying his wife was not home when he arrived there and having no idea of where she was, he decided to take a walk. For no particular reason, he picked up a sack containing his .45 which was fully loaded along with an extra clip of ammunition. He said he was just walking along when all of a sudden he saw his wife seated in an automobile with another man. He walked in the direction of the car when the man started up the car and tried to run over him. That was when he took his pistol from the sack, stepped into a ditch, and started shooting. He did not remember reloading the pistol and did not know how many shots he fired but he had to step into a shallow ditch to avoid being run over and this was corroborated to some extent by the fact that there were tire marks in the ditch.

Hunt was about thirty years old and a nice looking fellow with a good reputation. One of the character witnesses we used was an elderly lady who ran a boarding house where Hunt had stayed prior to his marriage. The lady was an impressive witness, firm in her testimony. The trial was a rough-and-tumble affair. It was Dunaway's first big case since being elected Prosecuting Attorney and he was well-prepared and tried it in an able manner. Of course, he tried Hunt while I tried the deceased woman, the wife. She was strictly no good and one of the things I was able to show was that while Hunt was serving his country in France during World War II, she lived in Chicago with another man who used Hunt's name for check cashing purposes.

I always found that in the defense of a criminal case, if the jury could be kept in a somewhat light frame of mind by getting an occasional laugh, it was good for the defendant. There was something that happened a few days before the killings that I was able to get into evidence and it did get a laugh from some of the jurors. Hunt was painting the floor of one of the rooms of their apartment and his wife's cat came into the room getting paint on its feet. The cat licked its feet and got sick. The wife took the cat to a veterinarian where she left it overnight and when she went back the next morning, the cat was dead. She immediately rushed back to the apartment and furiously told Hunt, "You son-of-a-bitch, you killed my cat!"

The case was hard-fought and the trial resulted in a hung jury. They could not reach a unanimous verdict and, in the retrial, there was a verdict of not guilty. Considering the facts of this case, winning it was, again, winning against the odds!

There never was a trial for the killing of the man who was with Hunt's wife. When there is more than one crime growing out of the same act, the prosecutor usually selects his best and strongest case for trial. If he wins, there is no need for the other case to come to trial. If he loses, it is not likely he will win the weaker case and usually does not try.

Tom Poe, a lawyer and friend of mine, was trying an insurance case in Federal Court which involved injuries to the driver of a car which went into Fourche Creek west of Little Rock. The litigation involved a considerable amount of money. As one of the witnesses, Tom used an automobile mechanic who had worked on the car after it had been removed from the creek. He testified that a car of a certain make had been brought to him for repairs and that certain damages had been done to it. It developed that the automobile owned by the plaintiff was of a different make, a very important material point in the litigation.

After the case was over, the trial judge had the mechanic arrested for perjury. He was indicted and retained me to defend him. One reason I mention this case is because it is the only case I ever had where the charge was perjury. My defense in the trial was that the witness had not wilfully sworn to a lie, that when he testified he was merely confused and made a mistake in the make of the car. I presented a compelling reason why he might have done so.

The mechanic had served overseas in World War II and had been struck in the face by a splinter from an airplane propeller. This injury caused a condition known as "tic douloureaux." I proved by medical testimony that it is an extremely painful condition and that the treatment to relieve the pain is injection of alcohol into the nerve, although the drinking of alcohol will help to some extent.

The man testified that he had drunk so much alcohol over a period of time in an effort to keep down the pain, that he had become an alcoholic. He said he was at least partially under the influence of alcohol from morning until night, that he started drinking immediately after getting up every morning. But, on the day of the previous trial, he said he did not want to come to court the least bit under the influence of alcohol or even smelling of it. So he did not drink anything, the result being that he was not at all himself at the time he testified in the insurance case. The jury found the man not guilty.

I will mention one other case before I turn to my years on the Arkansas Supreme Court — the case of Billy Forby, a young man who was charged with the rape of a twelve-year-old school girl. I was retained to defend him by his uncle, a wealthy planter who lived in northeast Arkansas.

The little girl was on her way home from school when she was accosted by the defendant, taken into some nearby woods and raped. When Billy was arrested, he did not deny to the officers that he had had sexual intercourse with the little girl and his attitude was, "Well, what about it? I didn't do anything wrong."

When I got into the case, I found that Billy had a history of mental disorder. I got his army records which showed that in World War II he had been sent back from China to a hospital in California because of his mental condition. He later told me that when he was in China, it was common practice there to have sex with very young girls.

I also saw from the army records that he had been examined by a Dr. Beal who had diagnosed Billy as being Schizophrenic and who noted that he would soon break down into a "frank psychosis." I immediately began to trace down Dr. Beal and found he was an assistant superintendent of the Pennsylvania State Hospital in Morristown, Pennsylvania. But I located him in Washington, D.C. where he was giving examinations for admission to some psychiatric society.

I talked with him on the phone, telling him of the case and of his examination and diagnosis of Billy at Muroc, California. I prevailed upon him to come to Little Rock, examine Forby, and testify in the case if his findings were the same as before. Dr. Beal did come to examine Forby, reporting that he was even worse than before and said he would testify to such facts.

Dr. Beal appeared as a witness in the jury trial to determine if Forby was sane enough to stand trial on the rape indictment. The issue to be decided was Forby's present mental condition, sane or insane. When I put Dr. Beal on the stand, I showed his qualifications which were extensive, his examination of Forby as recorded in the army records, then the recent examination in Little Rock. I asked Dr. Beal's opinion as to whether Forby was sane or insane and received the reply that Forby was insane. I then asked him the basis for his opinion. Dr. Beal talked for four hours and had the attention of everyone in the very quiet courtroom. When he finished, I said, "That's all. No further questions."

Dunaway, the Prosecuting Attorney, took Dr. Beal on cross- examination and tried to show that some of his testimony was in conflict with a recognized textbook on the subject. Dunaway picked up a book from the table, opened it to a marked page, and asked Dr. Beal if he was familiar with the textbook, *Norris on Psychiatry*. Dr. Beal quickly ended Dunaway's attempt to discredit him. "Yes," he replied, "my superintendent wrote it and I helped him. " Dr. Norris just happened to be the superintendent at the Pennsylvania State Hospital where Dr. Beal was the assistant superintendent and the institution is recognized world wide as one of the greatest of its kind. Dr. Norris was recognized in a like manner. Dunaway made no further reference to the book.

Another thing I was able to bring out during the trial was that, when Forby was sent from Muroc, California, to the government hospital at Memphis, he was able to visit his aunt and uncle in Arkansas while on furlough. His aunt recognized that Forby was totally insane and that he should be confined to a hospital. When the authorities at the Memphis hospital were about to release Forby, she unsuccessfully tried to keep them from granting the release.

When the case was submitted to the jury, that body promptly returned a verdict of insanity. Under this verdict, Forby would be confined to the Arkansas State Hospital for Nervous Diseases until such time as the superintendent of that facility would file in court, a certificate to the effect that Forby had recovered sufficiently to stand trial on the rape charge.

Dr. Jackson, the State Hospital Superintendent, along with several other doctors on the hospital staff, had testified at Forby's trial that he was sane. They were furious at the verdict of insanity. Forby had not been in the State Hospital more than a few weeks when a certificate of sanity was filed in court. I tried to block a second trial with an appeal to the Arkansas Supreme Court, but was unsuccessful. Forby was to stand trial on the rape charge again.

The father of the rape victim had been hell-bent on Forby going to the electric chair. He retained Pat Mehaffy, a former Prosecuting Attorney, and Otis Nixon, one of my deputies when I was Prosecuting Attorney, to assist the prosecutor. I understand he paid them handsome fees. But the rape trial was practically a duplicate of the insanity trial. This time, however, there was a verdict of guilty and a life sentence. Forby's relatives and I were satisfied with the verdict as I had offered to plead Forby guilty and take a life sentence to start with. We knew his mental condition would not improve and that he would have to be confined somewhere for the rest of his life. We all felt it was better for him to be at the penitentiary which had twenty thousand acres of farmland, including a very large garden. There he would be placed in a job suitable to his condition. At the State Hospital he would have just been locked up.

Chapter XVII

The Supreme Court and Beyond

In the year 1950 there were two vacancies on the Arkansas Supreme Court that were to be filled in the statewide general election. I wanted Jack Holt, Sr. to run for one of the two positions. He had served as a Circuit Judge, as Attorney General of the State, and would have made a splendid Supreme Court Justice. He had run for Governor two years previously but had been defeated by Sid McMath.

At that time I made quite a few speeches for him around the state. His son, Jack Holt, Jr., then about eighteen years of age, drove me to these speaking engagements. Later, Jack, Jr., became a lawyer and after enjoying a successful practice for a number of years, was himself, elected chief Justice of the Supreme Court and now serves in that capacity. But Jack did not want to run. He was not on good terms with Sid McMath, who was then Governor, fearing Sid might be against him and could bring about his defeat. I thought that Sid would be looking after his own business of running for re-election and would not meddle in Jack's race for the Supreme Court, but I could not convince Jack on this point.

Witt Stephens, a friend of mine, was the most powerful figure in Arkansas politics and was a friend of McMath. I talked the matter over with Witt and he agreed to help me get Jack to run, so I got a room at the Albert Pike Hotel there in Little Rock and made arrangements for Jack and me to meet with Witt.

At this meeting we had a thorough discussion of the situation, but Jack was still adamant in thinking that Sid would use his influence against him if he were to become a candidate. Finally, the discussion got kind of heated and Jack turned to me, saying, "If you are so damn sure that Sid won't meddle in the race, why don't you run?" I said, "If Witt here will support me, I will!" Witt said, "I'll support you." And I said, "I'm running." That is how I got into the race for a position on the Arkansas Supreme Court.

At that time, lawyers did not make a whole lot of money. To illustrate, my salary as Prosecuting Attorney had been five thousand dollars per year. So I did not have much money with which to campaign. But it so happened that both of my opponents in the race, Charlie Wine of Texarkana and Leffel Gentry of Little Rock, were somewhat in the same boat.

In the very first part of the campaign, we all happened to be at a political meeting up in the northern part of the state, I think it was Batesville. And although each of us was campaigning as hard as we could, we were still friends. The three of us were discussing the campaign and got around to talking about finances and finally hit on the idea that we could campaign without spending any money on advertising and each of us would have just as good a chance as the other. We made an agreement to that effect, that we would do no advertising; no radio, no newspapers, no posters, no billboards, just word of mouth. And of course, this cut the campaign expenses to a nominal amount. I worked hard to be elected, going to every town and city in the state and seeing as many people as I possibly could.

In Arkansas, a candidate must receive a majority of all the votes cast in order to be elected. If no candidate receives a majority during the regular election, the top two candidates run in a second election held about two weeks later. I led the ticket in the regular election but did not get a majority vote. Wine received the least votes, leaving Gentry and me to run it off, which I won by a majority, more than thirty thousand votes. Judge Paul Ward, Chancery Judge at Batesville, was elected to the other vacancy and we were to be sworn in on January 1, 1951 at the regular meeting of the court.

A justice of the State Supreme court holds one of the highest positions within the gift of the people, and it is something of which one can be very proud. The morning I was to be sworn in, many of my friends and relatives were present in the courtroom and the same applied to Judge Ward.

Judge Griffin Smith was Chief Justice and, as such, he was in charge of opening and closing of the Court. He was very punctual. All the judges would gather in a hall to the rear of the courtroom and Judge Smith would have his watch in his hand. At the very second it read nine o'clock, he opened the door and all the judges marched in and took their place on the bench.

On the morning in question when it came time to open court, newly-elected Ward was not there. At exactly nine o'clock Judge Smith opened the door and we all marched in, without Judge Ward. His many friends and relatives were horrified and could not guess what had happened. Judge Smith swore me in, I took my place on the bench with the other judges, and we took up the business at hand. About ten minutes later Judge Ward showed up. Judge Smith swore him in and things proceeded smoothly.

It turned out that Judge Ward had a bad habit of being late for meetings of all kinds. This had been his habit over the years and apparently he couldn't help it. But thereafter, he did help it, at least insofar as the opening of Court was concerned. He was never late again. He would be late for conferences sometimes, but not for the opening of Court.

Being a Supreme Court Judge would only appeal to those really interested in the law. The job requires studying law day and night, in solitude, day after day, year after year. When a judge is not listening to oral arguments, he is reading briefs prepared by lawyers, reading law or writing law. Otherwise, a Supreme Court Justice's life is wrapped up in the law.

A typical day consisted of my getting to the office about 8:30 a.m., speaking for a moment to my stenographer and law clerk, and then retiring to my private office to write opinions or work on a case to be written. I usually left my office about 4:30 in the afternoon and went home. After supper I read briefs until about 10 p.m. There was very little visiting between the judges. We were too busy for that. We worked all the time.

Oral arguments were heard every Monday morning in the court room, followed by a conference of the Justices who would discuss all of the cases to be decided that day. The Clerk of the Court also assigned new briefs for that week, with each of us writing one or sometimes two opinions, those cases to be decided on the following Monday.

Sometimes judges would exchange cases that they would write because for some reason, one of the judges did not want to write the case assigned to him. On one occasion, Chief Justice Griffin Smith, while I was in his office, asked me to make such a swap with him in a case that he had. I had not seen the briefs but I saw what appeared to be a one volume transcript (the ordinary size) and I agreed to the exchange. Later, when he brought the transcript to my office, it consisted of seven volumes and there was a 'question of fact' involved; otherwise, was the evidence sufficient to support the verdict. This meant a careful search of the transcript from the beginning to the end and it would take several times as long to write an opinion in this case than in an ordinary case. We just laughed.

I enjoyed my service on the Court. It was pleasant work and the companionship of the other judges was most agreeable. I wrote about six hundred majority opinions while I was on the Court; good, bad, or indifferent, they speak for themselves. And of course, I wrote some dissenting opinions, but not many. I usually helped make up thc majority opinion and these opinions appear in Volumes 218 to 240, *Arkansas Reports*, inclusive.

Some of these cases of first impression or considerable impact, come to mind. One is *Swagger v. State, 227 ARK 45*. This case was decided in 1956, years before the Civil Rights Act was adopted by Congress.

"On the night of April 13, 1956, S.R. Cady was shot and seriously injured. He was in his home, and the shot was fired through a window from the outside. The next morning, April 14, Swagger (a Negro youth of 19) was arrested. On Friday, April 20, the Prosecuting Attorney filed an information in Circuit Court charging him with assault with intent to kill. Monday morning,

April 23, the defendant pleaded guilty to the information and was sentenced to 21 years in the penitentiary."

After the defendant started serving his sentence, George Howard, an able black lawyer from Pine Bluff, and now a U.S. District Judge at Little Rock, was retained to see what could be done for Swagger. He filed a motion in Circuit Court in Pine Bluff alleging that Swagger had not had the benefit of due process of law because no attorney had been appointed to defend him. The motion was over-ruled and there was an appeal to the Supreme Court. It happened to fall my lot to write the case.

We held that,

In the case at bar, appellant did produce evidence as to the circumstances surrounding his plea of guilty. It was shown that he is a Negro boy, nineteen years of age, and is practically illiterate although his petition alleges he had gone to school; that he lives with an aunt 68 years of age; that during the few days he was held in jail, between the time he was arrested and the time he entered a plea of guilty, his aunt tried to visit him, but the jail authorities would not permit her to do so. True, the Prosecuting Attorney told the defendant while he was in jail that on a plea of guilty he would get him a sentence of 21 years in the penitentiary. But, it appears that perhaps the accused did not know that 21 years was the maximum sentence he could receive. In fact, the record indicates that the accused may have thought that he could be sentenced to a longer term of imprisonment.

We said in the opinion,

The petitioner is not entitled to his absolute freedom, but it is ordered that the judgment and sentence on his plea of guilty be set aside and that he be placed in the custody of the Sheriff of Jefferson County that appropriate proceedings against him may be taken.

Swagger had a new trial and was found guilty, this time by a jury, and was again sentenced to 21 years in the penitentiary. But he was paroled after serving much less time.

Another case, *The Little Rock Junior College v. the George W. Donaghey Foundation, 224 ARK. 895,* has had considerable influence on educational opportunities in the Little Rock area.

The case involved the construction of the will of Governor George W. Donaghey. Gov. Donaghey had set up a trust for the benefit of the Little Rock Jr. College, a two year school. Some years after his death, the college wanted to expand their program to become a four year college. The Chancery Court in Little Rock held that under the terms of the will, the money generated for the school could only be used for a two year college. The college contended that it could expand without losing their benefit under the will. The case was appealed to the Supreme Court and there the Court was sharply divided on the interpretation of the will.

I wrote the case. Three judges sharply dissented, each one writing a dissenting opinion. But two of the judges joined me absolutely, and a third concurred, making four voting for the four year construction. Due to the holding in that case, the Little Rock Jr. College was able to become a four year college, and eventually a branch of the University of Arkansas.

There was the case of *Missouri Pacific Transportation Co. v. Miller, 227 ARK. 351*, which I wrote. In that case, one of the principal issues was whether a wife was entitled to recover damages by reason of the loss of consortium with her husband, where the husband was totally disabled as a result of a bus accident in which they were passengers. I wrote,

Consortium has been defined as: the comfort and the decent and proper enjoyment of the affection of her husband; conjugal society; the society of her husband; the mass of indefinable duties and rights are conveniently gathered under the word consortium.

At that time the weight of authority both in this country and in England, was that the wife could not recover for loss of consortium although a husband could. The Arkansas Supreme Court had not passed on the point. But Sid McMath and Henry Woods, now a United States District Judge, had convinced the trial court and also convinced us, that the wife was entitled to recover. We held in favor of the wife and this case pretty well established everywhere the right of the wife to recover and the case has been cited many times by both state and federal courts, including United States Supreme Court. Forty one states have now adopted the rule that the wife can recover for the loss of consortium with her husband and it is now the majority rule. In fact, the case was a big boost to the rights of women.

Arkansas is extremely fortunate to have had George Rose Smith as one of its Supreme Court Justices. He was on the bench during my tenure and retired January 1, 1987. I returned to Arkansas by invitation and made a little talk at the retirement ceremony. The following is from the remarks I made at that time:

Judge Smith has all the qualities of a great Judge. He is the soul of honor, he has a brilliant mind, he is dedicated to the law, has a burning desire to keep the law straight, and is prejudiced against no one, regardless of his race, color or creed. And another point that should be mentioned, he is not lazy. And his capacity for remembering the law, the points decided, is astounding. Since he has been on the Court, the Court has handed down thousands of decisions, perhaps around ten thousand, and I venture to say he remembers all the points decided, and the style of the case in many of the most important ones.

After fifteen years, I decided I would like to get back to the practice of law. I was eligible for retirement as of January 1, 1966, and the previous fall I picked that day as my last on the Court.

Orval Faubus was Governor then and it was up to him to appoint someone to serve out my unexpired term. I went to him and told him of my intention to retire. He also had decided to retire, having already served several terms as he was very popular. After some conversation between us, Governor Faubus asked me if I would run for governor. With his backing and that of Witt Stephens, who was still a powerhouse in Arkansas politics, there would be no doubt about my being elected and I really would not have minded being governor. But I never wanted to be an ex-governor; I rather wanted to get back to the private practice of law.

On my last day, the first Monday in 1966, there was a large crowd in the courtroom and the Court presented me with a bronze plaque, which hangs in my living room and of which I am very proud. Courtney Crouch, representing the Arkansas Bar Association, and Bill Eldridge of the Little Rock Bar Association, both made speeches in my honor and presented me with a bound manuscript of those speeches, now in the possession of my daughter, Lucile (Mrs. Henry Johnson of Little Rock). I was very flattered by these tributes.

I practiced for seven years after retiring from the Supreme Court, but not in the practice of criminal law as I had done before. It was while I was on the Court that my friend Witt Stephens had purchased the Arkansas-Louisana Gas Company, commonly referred to as ArkLa. I tried two very important cases on behalf of his company.

I was one of the lawyers on a rate case before the Arkansas Public Service Commission seeking, among other things, to set aside a contract ArkLa had with the Arkansas Power and Light Company. The price of gas had greatly increased since the contract had been signed, and if it could not be set aside ArkLa would sustain a great loss — about twenty-two million dollars. We won that case.

The other case concerned the ownership of a tract of land bordering the Arkansas River near Fort Smith. The issue was whether the property was an island or accretion to the mainland owned by ArkLa. Accretion is a term used in civil law to denote an increase in property by fortuitous circumstances without cost to the owner, as an increase of land by flood or alluvial deposit. If the land was deemed accretion, it belongs to ArkLa; if adjudged to be an island, it belonged to a party who had purchased it as an island from the state. Gas under the surface of the parcel was valued at seven hundred and fifty thousand dollars.

The case had been tried once and the court had ruled that the land was an island and, therefore, belonged to the man who had bought it from the state. When I got into the case, I found that the judge had failed to sign the judgment and that this judge had left the bench. He, therefore, had no jurisdiction and could not then sign the judgment. There was nothing to do but to retry the case. But this time Heartsill Reagan, an attorney from Fort smith, and I tried the case and won it, the court holding the land was accretion to the property of the Arkansas-Louisana Gas Company.

When Sid McMath was Governor, Henry Woods, now a United States District Judge in Arkansas, was with him in the governor's office and he was McMath's right-hand man. After the Governor left office, he and Woods formed a law partnership, moved from Hot Springs to Little Rock, where they opened a law office and became the foremost trial lawyers in the state. Their success was phenomenal. They tried many personal injury cases and they took me in on quite a few of them. We never lost a case.

Supreme Court of Arkansas
1961

Sam Robinson, Paul Ward, Jim Johnson
George Rose Smith, J. Seaborn Holt, Carlton Harris, Ed F. McFaddin

Chapter XVIII

"Cub Cat"

During my years on the Supreme Court, I leased part of a large tract of government land along the Arkansas River that now makes up the town of Maumelle. The Court adjourned during the hot summer months and I had time to work with horses and cattle. The part I leased for my cattle was separated from an army facility by a high cyclone fence. On the army side of the fence was a road with a wooden bridge that crossed a ravine.

One morning two of my employees were going down the road in a pickup on their way to check on the cattle when a doe ran out in front of them onto the wooden bridge, where she slipped and fell and couldn't get up. The Major in charge of the facility was very strict about the deer not being harmed in any way; in fact, there hadn't been any hunting there for years. So my two cowboys went to headquarters to notify the Major.

They then went to get their horses and when they rode back, they were on the other side of the fence. Meanwhile, the Major and a Sergeant had come to see about the doe. Just as the boys arrived, a big ten-point whitetail buck deer walked out of the woods toward where the Major and the Sergeant were standing beside their vehicle.

When a whitetail buck gets used to the presence of people, it can become dangerous. And as the buck got closer, it became evident to everyone that he was going to attack. The Sergeant jumped in the car but the Major's only recourse was to grab the buck by the horns as it came at him. As he struggled with the deer the Sergeant got back out of the car to help. Then the Major jumped in with the Sergeant right behind, followed by the deer. The buck tore up the upholstery, but the two men were not injured and they managed to kick the buck out of the vehicle. He went on his way, but deer season was not too far off and I know there was one less buck on the army facility a few days after the season opened.

I had a nice little ranch west of Little Rock on Stagecoach Road, right near the Saline County line, about forty miles from the racetrack at Hot Springs. In addition to my home, my place had good facilities for training horses; thirty-four box stalls, an arena, and a half-mile track. I had been raising and training quarter horses there for years.

One morning Harold Tinker, a trainer, showed up there and wanted to know if I would break some thoroughbred yearlings and get them ready for the track. I told him I had never handled thoroughbreds but he looked over my barn, my quarter horses, and the other facilities and said he thought I could do it. He was willing to pay a whole lot more per horse per day than I had ever thought about receiving. I had to make only slight modifications in removing the wooden feed trough and hay mangers from the stalls.

At the time, Tinker was training for a man from St. Louis, but later on he became the trainer for Cal Partee. After I started breaking thoroughbred yearlings (most of them having been purchased at the Keeneland, Kentucky summer sale), I received yearlings from several sources, but by far the best and most satisfactory owner was Cal Partee. Cal sent me a lot of expensive yearlings. As I said, I had good facilities and good help and although I handled many yearlings, I had only one bad experience, this with one of Cal's yearlings.

This was at a time when I was on the Supreme Court and could only be at my ranch part time. But I had Dub Grant, a fine young man and an able horseman, as my foreman. On one occasion however, I hired a man from Florida as an exercise boy. He was the right size, looked okay, and after having him ride a horse in the arena, I hired him. After he had been there a while, someone left a pair of bull riding spurs hanging in the tack room. These spurs have very sharp rowels and, although they will not cut a bull's hide, they can really cut up a horse. One day in my absence, this man put on those spurs and before Dub Grant knew what was happening, he badly marked a yearling Cal had purchased at Keeneland for twenty-five thousand dollars. I arrived soon after the incident and it wasn't long before Cal arrived. I immediately told him what had happened. He looked at the horse and merely said, "He'll be all right." Many owners of a horse of that caliber would have had a spasm. That exercise boy never rode another horse for me.

Cal Partee is one of the finest sportsmen I have ever known. He still has his stable of horses and races them at the better tracks, and in fact, went on to win the Kentucky Derby in 1992. Cal bets on his horses and, win or lose, one cannot tell the difference by his actions or demeanor. He can lose a big race which would put an ordinary person in a terrible mood, but not Cal. He can take twenty-five people to dinner that night and still be the life of the gathering.

Colonel Gus Busch, Jr. of St. Louis was a friend of mine and an expert horseman and rider in every category of horsemanship. He owned a nice brick stable at Hot Springs that had been used for horses when wagons were used to deliver beer prior to the advent of the automobile.

Gussie, as he was called by his close friends, would come to Hot Springs occasionally, usually by rail in his private car. I wish he hadn't sold that car, it was really something and I don't think he needed the money. I stayed in the car one night after we had been on a big party and Gussie left a servant there to look after me although I don't know where Gussie stayed. Maybe he just continued to party after I gave out.

As an Arkansas Supreme Court Justice, I had the authority to perform marriages. Gussie was getting married to a young lady who was, I think, from Switzerland and wanted me to marry them at Hot Springs. A wedding breakfast preceded the ceremony with many of Gussie's relatives and friends in attendance.

I was seated next to Mrs. Anheuser and she told me she was having considerable pain in her shoulders caused by bursitis. I had treated this condition in myself and several friends, including my mother-in-law, with a horse liniment known only as "white liniment". In every instance in which I have used it, and I still do, it has cured the trouble. I told Mrs. Anheuser about it and suggested that she probably would not want to use it because it was, in fact, horse liniment. She said she had gotten to the point where she would try anything and I told her I would send some to her in St. Louis.

Later I dismissed the matter from my mind as I did not think she would really use horse liniment. But it wasn't long until I received a note from her asking, "Where is the liniment?" I immediately sent her some of it and soon I received a nice letter from her telling me the liniment had worked just fine.

Gussie was an expert rider of cutting horses and had a real good horse named "Budweiser Bud" and he would bring this horse with him to Arkansas. He would come to my place near Little Rock about forty miles from Hot Springs and we and other friends would practice cutting cattle in my arena. I had one of the best cutting horses I or anybody had ever ridden. His name was Cub Cat. This horse would have had a good chance at being a world champion except that he had a bad fault of bucking once in a while. He was real stout and could really turn it on, but in California before I owned him, Cub Cat had killed a man by bucking him off onto some concrete, thus getting a very bad reputation. I bought the horse from Austin Frank, the mayor of Pine Bluff, who was a real good rider and who owned several good cutting horses.

One time when Gussie was at my place to do a little cutting, I was riding Cub Cat. He was beautiful, built just right, and Gussie wanted to ride him — which, of course, was okay with me. Gussie hadn't ridden him very long before he came up to me and said, "I've got to have this horse. How much?" I really did not want to sell Cub Cat. He had never bucked with me and I liked him better than any horse I had, but neither did I want to refuse Gussie. I was sure the horse had outgrown his bucking trait and was okay for anyone to ride so I thought the matter over and told Gussie that I would take six thousand dollars for Cub Cat. Gussie said, "I'm taking him home," and he took the horse back to Hot Springs that night.

About a week later Gussie was at my place again and had one of his employees with him, a man named Whitey, who at one time handled one of the big beer wagon teams. Cub Cat was along too. After they had been there a short while, Wes Grant, who was working for me, got me aside and said that Whitey had told him that Cub Cat had bucked with Gussie, but that he had ridden him out and was not hurt. I was surprised at the bucking and certainly did not want to have sold Gussie a bucking horse, although I knew he had a lot of courage and was not afraid to ride any horse. He was not afraid of anything, man nor beast.

I went to Gussie and told him I understood that Cub Cat had bucked with him and he said that was true. I told him I would return his money and he said, "Oh, no. You're not getting this horse back!" Gussie had found out what had made the horse buck. it was the back cinch and by leaving it off the saddle, Cub Cat wouldn't buck. I never use a back cinch on any saddle and that is why the horse had never bucked with me. Gussie took the horse back to St. Louis and he never bucked again. However, if the horse had bucked every day, Gussie would have kept him because he had the courage to ride any horse and he wanted Cub Cat. The fact that the horse bucked would not have scared him off — not at all!

A few years later, Gussie wrote me from St. Louis and told me Cub Cat was lame, saying he knew how much I thought of the horse and that he would give him to me if I would come for him. I sent a man to St. Louis the next morning to bring Cub Cat back to Little Rock. He was lame in his right front foot and I could not determine what the trouble was. The races were going on at Hot Springs at the time and I talked with a veterinarian friend of mine, Dr. Harthill, at the track about Cub Cat's lameness. Dr. Harthill was considered the leading track veterinarian in the United States and said that if I would send the horse over to the track, he would get together with some other track vets and hold a clinic.

This was done and the diagnosis was "ringbone". Nothing could be done about his condition except to "nerve" the affected area; that is, certain nerves could be severed, relieving the pain that caused the lameness, but it would also cause the horse to eventually lose his hoof. I could not do this, so Cub Cat was used only occasionally.

Finally after practicing law for about seven years following my tenure on the bench, I retired and moved back to my old home in Lake Village, but I did not stay there long. My hunting trips to Colorado had given me a love for the mountains and the big outdoors.

Judge Sam Robinson, Outfitter

Chapter XIX

Colorado - New Adventures

I moved to Ouray County, Colorado, in the Rocky Mountains about 1973, buying a home on a small parcel of land on Log Hill Mesa. The view from my living room of the San Juan Mountains with snowcapped peaks about fourteen thousand feet high was simply magnificent.

I decided to go back into the cattle business in a small way and I bought one hundred and seventy-five head of yearlings from Perry Flanagan and Joe Baldwin, also leasing a fifteen hundred acre pasture from them. I leased this pasture for several years and their was never a scratch of a pen between us, never a misunderstanding or controversy.

The hunting is also great in southwestern Colorado and I had a hunting business which I ran with the help of my wife, Ruth Ann. We met and married a few years after I moved there. Ruth Ann is from New York but she has the nerve of a high diver and quickly learned to ride a horse real well.

I wanted to get a good horse for Ruth Ann — an outstanding horse and my friend, Wyatt Smith, an old-time cowboy, had what appeared to be such a horse. I had learned a long time ago to buy a horse only after having tried him out for about two weeks. There can be many things wrong with a horse that cannot be detected by merely looking him over or seeing him ridden in a sale ring; especially if he is being ridden by what appears to be an ordinary farm girl, but actually, she is an expert rider. And a horse may have many vices — some of which show up only occasionally, such as "balking."

A "balky" horse may be ridden a week or more without showing this very undesirable trait and then for no apparent reason, he "balks", and nothing will make him move. I learned a way to make a "balky" horse move, and after a few treatments, cure this vice. And that is, to throw him down by tying up one front leg and pulling his head around to where he becomes overbalanced and falls. Then, tie his head to the saddle horn in the twisted-back position and just let him lay there for quite a while; fifteen minutes or more as he can't get up. When you let him up, ride him off. It will probably be some time before he "balks" again and, after a few treatments, in all probability he will quit that bad habit.

Another bad vice that some horses have that cannot be detected readily is that of "pulling back." The horse may be tied up many times over a period of a week or more and stand there tied in a perfectly normal manner. Then one day he decides to "pull back" and will, all of a sudden, back up with all of his weight and strength usually until something breaks. And if nothing breaks, he will often throw himself to the ground, damaging the saddle or actually injuring himself. There is a way to cure this but, after all, I'm not writing a book about training horses. There are other vices equally as bad.

I bought the horse from Wyatt on two weeks trial and during this time Ruth Ann rode him and he appeared to be real good. He was a beautiful sorrel just the right size and had a good way of going. One day we rode to the pasture about five miles from our house to move steers from one section to another. The horse travelled just fine and we thought that he was what we wanted.

When in the pasture, we gathered together about eighty head of steers. It had been necessary for us to get out of sight of each other in doing this, but I told Ruth Ann to bring the steers on down a narrow canyon and that I would get out on top, ride to the other end and open a gate through which we wanted to drive the steers. I did this and waited.

In due time, Ruth Ann arrived with the steers and they were put through the gate. Ruth Ann's horse was white with sweat. He was really lathered and she said that just as soon as I got out of sight, the horse became really agitated, cutting up and nickering, and it was hard to do anything with him. She had gotten the steers down the canyon only because there was nowhere else for them to go. It was all she could do to control the horse and keep him coming down the canyon behind the steers.

Just as soon as the horse got back with my horse, he was perfectly calm again. He was what I refer to as a "buddy horse." He's all right as long as he is with some other horse, but when he is taken off by himself, he acts as I have described.

Ruth Ann and I ate a little lunch and rode on back to the house. When we got to the entrance of our place, I told Ruth Ann to ride my horse on in the gate and go to the barn, that I was going to ride her horse on down the road. I had gone not over a hundred feet when that horse decided he was not going any further and proceeded to let me know it in no uncertain terms. I knew that he was not only buddy-spoiled, but also barn-spoiled. I didn't want that horse, but had found it out only after having the horse and using him for about a week. I took the horse back to Wyatt who took him saying that he knew he was a little bit that way, but hadn't him long and didn't know the extent of his bad habits and didn't want us to have him either.

Back in Arkansas I had ridden cutting horses for years, belonged to the National Cutting Horse Association and owned some good cutting horses. For about two or three months during summertime, when the Supreme Court was on vacation, I got a great deal of pleasure out of going to cutting horse contests not only in Arkansas, but also in several adjoining states.

But I decided that I was going to take up head and heel roping. I, therefore, began looking for a horse trained in that respect. I have a friend in Denver, Ed Honen, whom I knew participated in that sport and was real good at it and I called him to see if he knew where I could buy a horse like I wanted. Ed said he knew of such a horse that was for sale, and that the horse was good in heading and heeling. He had been at a contest about a week before and a roper had won riding that horse. Ed did not pretend to know anything else about the horse.

I went to look at the horse several hundred miles from my place and I never got fooled so badly in all my life. The horse was of the right age, size and conformation, and was perfectly sound. I rode him around the premises there and roped a practice dummy a few times. The price was right and violating my practice of not buying a horse without trying him for about two weeks, I bought that horse there on the spot.

I had my horse trailer with me and brought the horse home. He was a good horse in the arena when heading or heeling, he could do either well. But when you've said that, you've said it all! He was not much good for any other purpose and, in addition, had the very bad habit of pulling back on occasion. We called this horse Barney, and he seriously injured me on two occasions.

At one time I was out looking for cattle just sitting loose in the saddle and riding slowly along a mountain road with John Martin. John was a good cowboy and expert in quarter horse bloodlines, and was working for me at the time. Suddenly without any warning whatever, my horse lunged forward as if coming out of a roping box. This action jerked me over the cantle and off the horse. The spur on my left foot caught in a heavy saddlebag and everything held fast with my head near the ground at the horse's feet. The horse did not run or kick, just started spinning rapidly. Finally, my foot came out of my boot and I hit the ground. I ended up with a broken collarbone, but John said later that he thought I was dead. At age seventy-eight, I was still winning against the odds!

I should have gotten rid of that horse then and there, but I didn't. That winter in my corral he was attacked by a mountain lion. He received cuts on the shoulder but for some reason, the lion quit him before doing further damage. At another time, a lion got into my corral and caused seventeen head of horses to break the fence down. We found the horses over a mile from home.

The following summer while again riding Barney, Ruth Ann and I were in a pasture where there were several loose horses. They all came toward us in a dead run. I tried to cut them off to keep them from getting around Ruth Ann's horse but Barney started bucking. He threw me off and came down on my left arm just above the elbow causing severe injuries from which I carry the scars to this day. That was the last time I ever rode that horse and I traded him for a mare. When Ruth Ann took me to the hospital it was later said that my chief concern was to make sure that she took care of my spurs and not let them get away.

Ruth Ann and I decided to take a trail ride over what is known as Rainbow Trail with the Graves family. We took along Ruth Ann's son, Chris, who was about eight years of age at that time. I was eighty. We rode our own horses having a nice little sorrel mare for Chris to ride. The ride lasted about a week starting at Salida and going south to the Great Sand Dunes, a distance of about one hundred and twenty-five miles. It was the nineteenth year that the Graves had conducted this ride and there were close to eighteen riders in our party.

One night we camped at a campground maintained by the U.S. Forest Service and it had an outhouse constructed of wood. It was a couple hundred yards from where our tent was located and during the night I had to go there. Somehow I got turned around and could not locate our tent and had to start calling for Ruth Ann to come and get me. I do not know how many people I woke up, but it was quite a deal. The next morning bear tracks were discovered all around the outhouse and over my tracks. I do not know when the bear was there but I'm glad we didn't meet.

Later, Ruth and I decided to put in a similar trail ride. We lived about one hundred miles from the Rainbow Trail and were across the Continental Divide over on the western slope of the Rockies, so it did not interfere with the Graves' ride. There is a suitable trail along the San Juan range in the National Forest called the "Dallas Trail," a beautiful place to ride. We got a permit to use the trail to conduct trail rides, acquired the necessary horses and equipment, and went into business. We rode from "Last Dollar Road" on the west to near Ouray, Colorado, on the east, a three-day ride.

For a while we also rented out horses and, on one occasion, we rented horses to the family of Ronn Mayer. They wanted to ride to the Blue Lakes near the top of Mt. Sneffels, about fourteen thousand feet high. They started their ride at the base of the mountain where we delivered the horses in our four-horse trailer and returned to the base about dusk the same day.

We had to make two trips to get our horses home that night and after returning to the mountain to get the second load of horses, it was about nine o'clock. From the base of the mountain to the hard-surfaced highway is about eight miles over a road that, for a ways, goes along the rim of a canyon where Dallas Creek runs. The road is partly graveled and partly just plain dirt. About the time we got the last four horses loaded, it started raining.

At one point where the road was just plain dirt, no gravel, there is a steep downgrade with a canyon on the right side of the road. It had rained just enough to make the road real slippery and the trailer started to slip and slide. Ruth Ann was driving, going less than ten miles per hour, and applying the brakes would have made things worse. The trailer jackknifed, fortunately going off the left side of the road, where it turned over on its left side. If the trailer had gone off the road on the right side with its heavy load of four horses, it would have pulled the truck over the canyon wall and we would have been falling 'til yet. The truck did not turn over but was still attached to the trailer whose wheels on the right-hand side were up in the air. This was winning against the odds!

The trailer had two compartments with two horses tied in each. The only divider to separate the horses was a gate between the front and rear compartments, and the horses were piled up on top of one another kicking and struggling desperately to get on their feet.

We had Bobby Dunham along with us, a sixteen-year-old wrangler who worked for us, son of our good friends, Don and Georgia Dunham. And Bobby proved himself a man that night.

The two horses in the front compartment, Morgan and Snip, were two of our biggest horses, each weighing about twelve hundred pounds. Ruth Ann climbed up on the side of the trailer and got the escape door open (facing skyward).

The horses were tied to posts with strong halters and lead ropes which a horse cannot break and, of course, they held fast inside the trailer. But Ruth Ann got my knife, crawled through the escape door into the trailer with the horses, and managed to cut both lead ropes. Now the following is unexplainable and unbelievable! She then managed to get each of the horses — big as they are — to climb out of that small escape door made only for a person.

In the meantime, Bobby and I were trying to get the other two horses, Sagehen and Blackie, both also good-sized horses, out the back door. However it happened, I will never know, but in getting the latch on the back door open with our bare hands, we actually broke the handle on the latch and got the door open.

Blackie struggled out of the trailer but Sagehen had somehow got turned around in the trailer with her head facing to the rear and was unconscious. About that time, a man and his wife drove up going to camp at the mountain and, with their aid, Bobby and I skidded the mare partway out of the trailer where she laid with her head on the ground still unconscious. She stayed in that position for quite a while, finally regained consciousness, struggled the rest of the way out of the trailer and to her feet.

Meanwhile, Ruth Ann had caught up Morgan and Snip and was holding them by what was left of the halter leads. All four horses appeared to be okay, no broken legs. We could not right the trailer, but we did manage to unhook it from the truck. It was decided that Ruth Ann and I would go and get our neighbor, Bob DeVeny, who has a four-horse trailer, to come get the horses. Bobby would lead the horses out as far as he could and meet us coming back with the other trailer.

There were several cattle guards on the road. A cattleguard is a framework of iron bars spaced several inches apart laid across a trench in a road. Ordinarily, cattle and horses will not cross them for fear of falling through them and getting their legs caught between the bars. They are effectively used on heavily traveled gravel roads as vehicles can easily drive over them. And there is always a gate next to it through which to move livestock, but the gates must be opened for them to pass through and then closed again. It was thought that Bobby would get along better in that situation by walking and leading the horses instead of riding one and leading three.

When we got to Bob DeVeny's house it was one o'clock in the morning and he and his wife, Betty, were in bed. When he was told of our predicament, he immediately got his rig and we went back after the horses.

Bobby had walked out to the highway with the horses by the time we returned, but he had encountered some more trouble on the way out. Somehow, one horse had fallen on his back in a narrow irrigation ditch. Bobby had one more terrible time getting him out of that ditch, but managed to do it. The horse's short lead rope, having been cut to get him out of the trailer, was tied up real short to the lead rope of another horse and that horse helped pull him over so he could get up. We got back home with the horses at three o'clock in the morning. Later that same day, in looking the horses over carefully, we could find no evidence of any injury except a little skin knocked off the back part of the horse's right front leg.

Bob DeVeny went with us again that day and we managed to get the trailer turned back over on its wheels and brought it on home. It had sustained little damage. Bob breaks horses as a full-time occupation and is an expert in that field. He is recognized throughout the area for his ability and usually had a waiting list of people who want him to break a horse. He usually has a horse going real good and gentled for most anyone to ride in about thirty days. And, incidentally, his wife, Betty, is a wonderful cook. She has cooked for us at our hunting camps.

Several years ago I bought a tall, good looking cream colored mule from my friend and neighbor, Wayne Flowers. Wayne is a rancher, having lived in this area all of his life and he has a hunting camp at the foot of Horsefly Peak. I first came to this country with Bo Eagle of Lonoke, Arkansas to hunt at Wayne's camp. We named this mule Moses and he was a jumper, in fact, he was such a good jumper that we put him in training. Chris, my stepson, was about ten years old at the time and he rode the mule while being trained in jumping.

Moses was a good pack mule as well as a good riding mule. On one occasion, Wayne wanted to use him at his hunting camp for packing in game. Since Wayne had owned the mule, he knew what a good pack animal he was. I let him have Moses and he took him to the hunting camp at Horsefly Peak, a distance of about ten miles over a 4x4 road. The next morning Moses was back home, having jumped six gates to get there. Wayne soon came after Moses and I said to him that perhaps he had better take a pack horse. We have several good ones, but he wanted the mule. He knew how good Moses was in packing freshly killed game. Wayne said that he thought that if he hobbled the mule and put him with some horses, he would stay at camp. So Ruth Ann rode Moses back to Wayne's camp that afternoon and Wayne hobbled him and put him in a pasture with his horses.

The next morning Ruth Ann, while walking out to the mailbox, met Moses coming up our driveway, his legs still hobbled! Moses had travelled the ten miles while jumping six gates, hobbles and all, to get back home again. This time we let him stay at home and gave Wayne a pack horse to use.

After owning Moses about eight years, we put him with some horses in a pasture we had rented. He got his right hind leg cut real bad between the ankle and the hoof and we did everything we could for him. The veterinarian even performed a major operation, but it was no use. He was crippled for life and always undergoing some pain and we had him put down.

In connection with our trail rides, we had acquired thirty-two head of horses and occasionally, when we did not have rides scheduled, we would rent horses to other outfitters. Scott MacTiernan, who operates the San Juan Guest Ranch in Ridgway, Colorado, was one of the outfitters to whom we rented horses. We would not rent them to just anyone. Scott had rides that started at Cunningham Gulch out from Silverton and also at Ironton, one of the few flat places between Ouray and Silverton.

The highway between Ouray and Silverton goes over Red Mountain Pass and this road is frightening to some of even the most experienced drivers on mountain roads. In many places it appears just a narrow trail swung on the side of a mountain.

In delivering the horses to MacTiernan at Cunningham Gulch and Ironton, Ruth Ann and I traveled this road pulling our horse trailer loaded with four horses. Often we had to make several trips to deliver the number of horses Scott wanted and sometimes this road would be wet and slippery and not only did it look dangerous, it was dangerous. People are killed every year by mishaps on this road. On one occasion we delivered some horses to Ironton when it was raining so hard it was difficult to see very far ahead. On another occasion, while crossing Red Mountain, we were almost blinded by the snow and there was nothing that could be done except to keep on going. One of those on one of Scott's rides was Hayden Fry, a friend of mine, who had coached football at a Texas University. For the past several years he has been head coach at the University of Iowa where he has made an outstanding record and has been recognized as "Coach of the Year."

After we had been conducting trail rides for a couple of years, we decided to go into Outfitting for deer and elk hunting. We were real fortunate in being able to acquire two permits in the Uncompaghre National Forest, one in the Beaver Creek area near Mt. Sneffels, the other along Cimarron Ridge, both in the San Juan range. There were several thousand acres in our permits.

Our main camp in the Cimarron Ridge country was at the elevation of ninety-two hundred feet and could only be reached by four-wheel drive vehicles. In 1984 we established another full-service camp that could not be reached by vehicle, about six miles north of our main camp. We had to pack in horseback and Bob DeVeny was in charge of that camp. There were people with us having a lifetime of experience in those mountains including Farrell Hawk and his son, Lee. Farrell was an experienced Outfitter, himself, and knew those mountains like a book.

We moved into camp on a Friday in the first part of October and there is usually very little snow at that time. In fact, on this occasion there was no snow on the ground. However, it started snowing Saturday and it did not let up. Lee killed an elk on Saturday but there was no use in trying to continue the hunt.

By Sunday the snow was between three and four feet deep and the elk left the area. The snow was more than belly deep to a horse, but Bob DeVeny had managed to ride from the pack-in camp the six miles to our camp. It was the opinion of everyone that we had better try to get out of there.

Having broken a trail between the two camps, Bob, along with one of our wranglers, took in enough horses to get the hunters and crew out from the second camp. This was done without incident but we had no chance of getting the camp out since the snow had drifted almost to the top of our five-foot wall tents, so we just let it stay as it was.

There were several four-wheel drive vehicles at our main camp and, with the help of some of our saddle horses and lariat ropes, everybody, including Max Brown, who was then Sheriff of Chicot County, Arkansas, and his wife, Ina, and Bill Drew, a leading lawyer of southeast Arkansas, and also Mike Roland, was either shoveling snow or pushing and we managed to get the vehicles and also our main camp out.

After we came out, it quit snowing and the weather cleared. In about two weeks, the snow had settled a great deal and we rented a helicopter with a pilot for $325 an hour to go in and get our camp that we had left behind. The helicopter had a big net swung below it and Bob DeVeny and one of our wranglers went in with the helicopter pilot and got everything out in two trips.

In our way of life there was always something unusual happening. There were few dull moments. One of these happenings was a time when it was fifteen below zero and Ruth Ann and I went to the little town of Colona to get a tank of water. At that time we did not yet have a well at our home, but later on we put one in. There are quite a few people around that country who do not have wells, but haul their water in 300 gallon tanks on pickup trucks from Colona, as Ruth Ann and I were doing at that time.

There is an overhead water outlet where the water is obtained and as I have said, it was fifteen below zero. I turned on the water to put it into our tank, stepped back, stumbled over some snow, and fell on my back. When I did this, I got a lap full of water from the faucet. I had on good, heavy wool pants and the water did not get through to my skin. But by the time we filled the tank and I went to get in the pickup, my pants were frozen stiff and I literally had to crack the ice at my knees and hips to get in the truck.

As I mentioned before, there are mountain lions in this area and during the night one of them killed forty-one of Wayne Flower's sheep. Men from the Division of Wildlife came out to investigate. They confirmed the fact that it was a lion that did the killing and they brought in some dogs but could not pick up the lion's trail.

About two weeks later, the lion again got into the sheep one night and killed nineteen more of them. J.B. Humphreys, who works for the Division of Wildlife and is recognized as one of the best hunters anywhere, came out with another man and his dogs. This time they picked up the lion's trail, tree'd it and because it was a sheep killer, they did not capture and relocate it, but killed it on the spot.

During one summer Ruth Ann and I agreed to take a group of veterinarians and their wives from the east, on a trail ride lasting three days and two nights. There were about fifteen in the party. First and last, just about everything went wrong.

We hauled our horses to where the Alpine Trail crosses the Little Cimarron River. We put up a tent at the Little Cimarron for Chris, then eleven years of age, and Blake Guffy, a neighbor boy, to stay all night with the horses. We came on back home to meet the riders the next morning and transported them to the Little Cimarron getting the riders and horses started in good shape by eight o'clock in the morning.

Ruth Ann guided the riders the first day across the Little Cimarron, took the Alpine Trail, and climbed to the top of what is known as High Mesa, travelling west. After crossing High Mesa, a considerable distance, the trail drops down to the big Cimarron River. After the ride got started, the camp crew drove back to Highway 50, a distance of about twenty miles, and then west to the big Cimarron and, thence, up the big Cimarron to where the Alpine Trail drops down off the High Mesa. Deborah, my sixteen year old step-daughter, was following us in a car.

We set up camp at that point. We had to put up six twelve-by-fourteen tents, unfold and set up canvas cots for everybody, prepare the Coleman lanterns, cookstove, and all the other paraphernalia it takes to make a good camp. But we got everything in good shape by the time the riders arrived from the Alpine Trail.

Ruth Ann cooked a good supper, the horses were taken care of properly, the riders were thoroughly enjoying themselves and had a good night's sleep. Everything so far had gone smoothly.

At that location, the Alpine Trail joins the Lou Creek Trail which goes over the Cimarron Ridge at Lou Creek Pass; ten thousand seven hundred feet. Ruth Ann had taken the wrangler, who was to lead the party, over the pass about a week before so that he would know the trail. But, on this occasion, after crossing the Cimarron River, he got confused and it took him quite a little while to find right trail. Some time was lost there.

Finally, he did get on the right trail and followed it over the pass which is kind of rugged. After crossing over the pass and getting to the bottom of the Ridge, Lou Creek Trail continues on to the west and, at a point, Deer Creek Trail takes off to the right and goes to the site of our main hunting camp. That was where the parties were supposed to go.

Meanwhile, we broke camp on the big Cimarron and were supposed to drive back to Highway 50, then to Montrose and, thence, to the campsite, a distance of about sixty miles. Ruth Ann drove the truck, while Deborah and Forrest Cooper followed us in the car. Forrest was the son of our close friends, Dave and Janice Cooper. They themselves are some of the best help you could ever hope to find, whether it be with livestock, vehicles, hunting, or just anything. And I always tell people that Janice has eyes like a chicken hawk. She sees everything and doesn't miss a trick.

We were supposed to have the camp set up by the time the riders arrived, but there were a series of mishaps. After crossing over Lou Creek Pass and getting to the bottom of the Ridge, which is a real adventurous ride, our wrangler missed the Deer Creek Trail and rode on to the west. He rode quite a distance before discovering that he was on the wrong trail and had to turn around and ride back to where he had missed the Deer Creek Trail. He finally found it and followed it to our campsite, getting there later that evening. We weren't there — there was no camp! Knowing that something was wrong, they rode on out.

We had the camp loaded in our truck and had driven to within about five miles of the campsite when we got hopelessly bogged down in a real soft place in the road. A spring had been seeping underground at that place and it was really boggy. Devan, our four-year-old granddaughter, got out of the truck and went down in the muck to her waist. Ruth Ann had to pull her out.

There was no chance of us moving the truck, it was completely bogged down to the fenders. It was still daylight at this time and so we sent Deborah and Forrest to walk the five miles to the campsite to let the riders know what had happened and tell them to ride on out. We had no chance of getting there with the camp. After walking about a mile, they came to a fork and took the wrong road. They walked about a mile on that road when they came across a bull. The bull started towards them and they climbed a tree and stayed quite a while until the bull left. I don't think the bull was after them, but they thought so.

We had left the car at the end of the gravel road about two miles back. Ruth Ann took Devan with her and walked back to the car with the intention of driving to Pat Burke's place to see if he would let us put our horses in his corral that night. Pat is employed by the State Division of Wildlife and has charge of a big area, including the winter feeding grounds for hundreds of elk.

By this time, it was quite late, but when Pat found out about our troubles, he volunteered to come and get our truck out of there. So, Ruth Ann drove on back to the end of the gravel road. In the meantime, I had walked out. A gate is located about a quarter mile from the end of the gravel road. When I got to this locked gate, the riders were there. They had gotten to that point just a little bit before I did. I opened the gate and the riders went on through to the end of the gravel road where we had our horse trailer parked.

Just about this time, Pat arrived with a huge backhoe and Ruth Ann went with him to get the truck out of the bog. Ruth ann said Pat, with this good backhoe, lifted the rear end of the truck up and backed out with it as if it were a toy. Ruth Ann turned it around and drove it back to the end of the gravel road.

It was decided that the riders would get in the horse trailer to ride back down the mountain. We unsaddled the horses and turned them loose except for three, which Chris and Forrest used, along with the wrangler, to bring the horses on down the road to Pat's corral. But there was one thing we overlooked — cattleguards! There were seven cattle guards on that road but before getting to the first one, the horses decided that they wanted no more of the road and took off to the brushy hills. Pat, who was coming along with the backhoe, caught a big buckskin that had on a halter with a lead rope around his neck.

Pat, riding bareback with only the halter and lead rope on the horse, took to the brush with Chris and Forrest to try and round up the horses. By this time, it was about midnight. The horses, although somewhat scattered, had stopped about a quarter of a mile from the road and they got the horses together in the dark and brought them back to the road where they took off in the right direction. But they hadn't gone very far when they came to a cattle guard constructed entirely of steel. It is unbelievable, but all of the horses jumped the cattle guard without getting caught in it except two, and one of those got out by himself in just a little bit. The other one, a mare named Silky, was down with all four legs caught in the cattle guard. Pat said that he would go on to his house, get a cutting torch, come back and cut the cattle guard so that the mare, Silky, could get out.

In the meantime, the wrangler and the boys had gotten ahead of the horses and were holding them up in the road. Pat, who had gotten back into his backhoe, also got ahead of them and stopped in the middle of the next cattle guard, blocking the road, and he opened the gate alongside the cattle guard so the horses could go through there. At this time, Chris and Forrest were holding the horses back pretty good. Pat went on down the road opening the gates alongside, blocking each cattle guard until the horses arrived.

In the meantime, I was back there at the cattle guard in which Silky was caught. And right while I was looking at her, somehow, in some manner that I can't explain, the mare made a big struggle, her legs came out of the cattle guard and she was on her side. She rolled over, her feet landed on the ground, and she got up. I caught her immediately after she got out of it and thought surely she would have one or more broken legs, but she hardly had a scratch. The horses were taken on down and put in Pat's corral for the night.

The veterinarians and their wives were staying in Ouray and we took them there in the horse trailer. These riders had been travelling mostly by horseback since about seven a.m. the previous morning and here it was after midnight. We finally got home at three a.m. and later that morning Ruth Ann went to Ouray to see that everything was okay with the riders. We refunded them part of their money, not at their request however, and everything was satisfactory.

Chapter XX

The Final Chapter

While in camp during the 1988 hunt, at an altitude of 9,200 feet, I developed a breathing difficulty. It was hard for me to get enough air. I was 89 years of age and my heart just could not pump enough oxygen at that altitude so I had to leave camp and go home. We lived at 7,900 feet altitude and even at that lower altitude, I continued to have trouble with my breathing. We realized that I could not continue to live there. This was in November of 1988, and in December we began the search for a new place to live.

After considering several places including a trip to San Antonio, Texas, to look at the situation there, we decided to move back to my old home, Little Rock. We sold our hunting outfit to Doug Flowers, the nephew of our good friend, Wayne, and gave up our hunting permits in the National Forest. In June of 1989, Ruth Ann, 3 cats, 4 horses and I moved to Arkansas. At age 93 I am comfortable, I still ride my horse, and I am still winning against the odds.

Index

...D...

...E...

...F...

...G...

...H...

...S...

...T...

...V...

...W...

...Y...